# ASHTAR'S
# THE SPACE BROTHERS SPEAK

## Transmissions From

## The

## Solar Council

# MEANING OF THE ASHTAR COMMAND SYMBOL.

*As if you took a stamp,*
*and marked a letter.*
*This is our sign,*
*to people on the Earth,*
*to know that we are here.*

## INNER LIGHT/GLOBAL COMMUNICATIONS

P.O. Box 753
New Brunswick, NJ 08903

mrufo8@hotmail.com

Art © by Carol Ann Rodriguez.

**THE SPACE BROTHERS SPEAK: TRANSMISSIONS FROM THE SOLAR COUNCIL**

**By The Ashtar Command and Their Earthly "Representatives"**

**Contributors:**
Timothy Green Beckley, Sean Casteel, Tuella, Hercules Invictus,
Marc Brinkerhoff, Carol Rodriquez

Published in the United States of America By
Inner Light/Global Communications
Box 753, New Brunswick, NJ 08903

**Staff Members**
Timothy G. Beckley, Publisher
Carol Ann Rodriguez, Assistant to the Publisher
Sean Casteel, General Associate Editor
Tim R. Swartz, Layout, Graphics and Editorial Consultant
William Kern, Editorial and Art Consultant

Sign Up For Our Free Weekly Newsletter and Mail Order Version of Conspiracy Journal and Bizarre Bazaar

www.ConspiracyJournal.com

Email: MrUFO8@hotmail.com

# CONTENTS

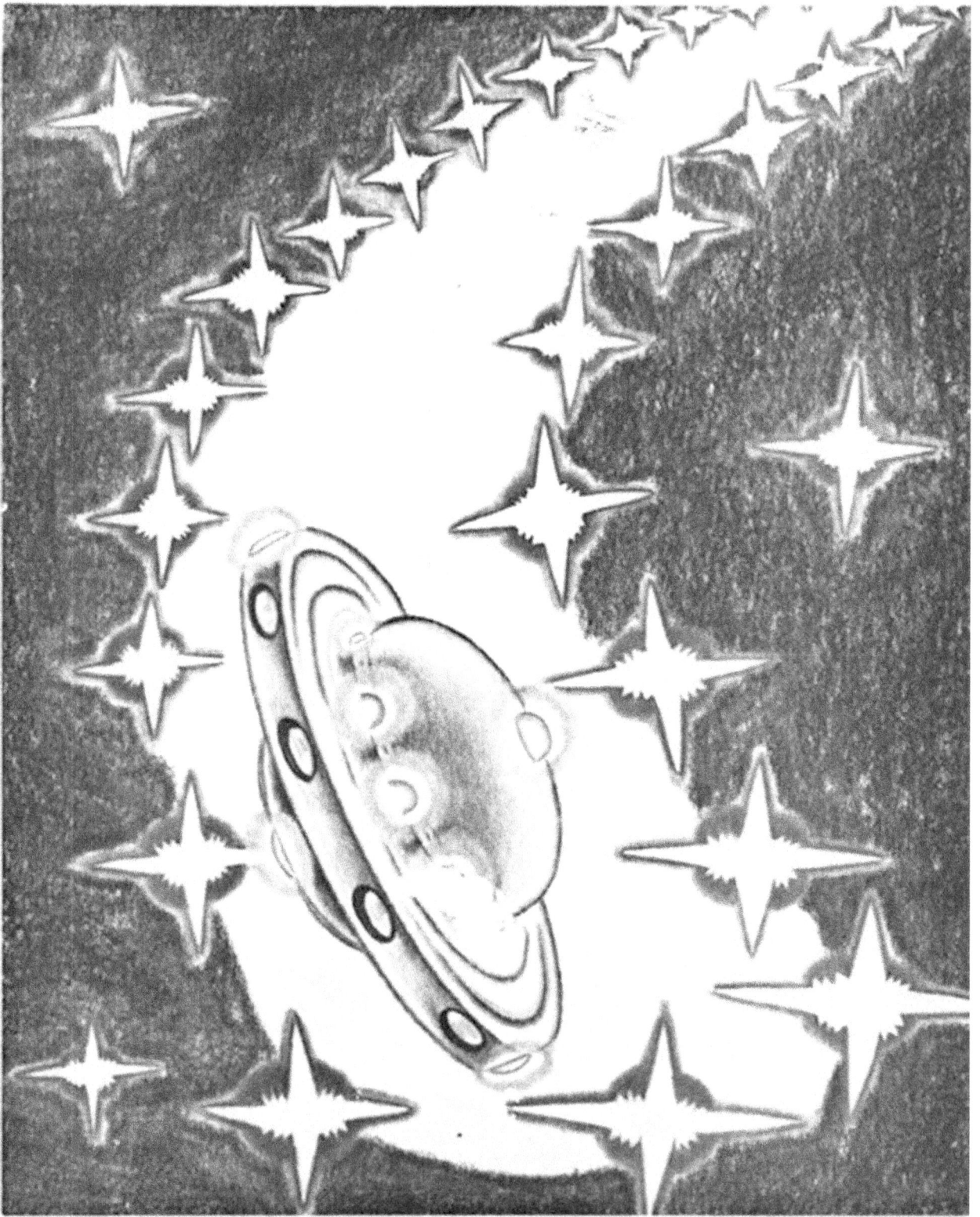

Art © By Carol Ann Rodriguez

## THE ASHTAR COMMAND WANTS YOU TO BE READY
## FOR THE COMING CHANGES TO TAKE PLACE SOON

They are not shy when it comes to making predictions or sometimes even making their "postulations" known. They can be subtle, but sometimes they are not – getting right to the point without mincing words – telepathically or not!

Depending upon the channel that is coming forth with a message, they have been known to draw attention to such vital matters as the:

- Future destiny of the Planet Earth.

- The coming arrival – in the form of mass landings – of their spaceships.

- The evacuation from our planet of the "worthy" to a safe new home in space.

- Signs and wonders in the heavens that will let you know when the "last days" have arrived.

- The rising of Atlantis and the reawakening of mankind into a new Golden Age.

### GOOD WILL AND GUIDANCE FROM OTHER WORLDS

Carol Ann, who has joyously worked alongside me for many years, having first entered my abode when she started attending lectures at my School of Occult Arts and Sciences back in the Seventies, mentioned recently that she thought our books were, to a degree, a bit too negative when it came to our "friends" from afar. She pointed out that our last few books have included such salacious titles as ***"Alien***

*Blood Lust*," "*UFO Hostilities*," and "*Screwed By The Aliens*," the latter about rape and molestation carried out by our Ultra-terrestrial visitors.

Being more into the philosophy of the Space Brothers, Carol waits for the return of the Ashtar Command to our cosmic shores – the Ashtar Command being a sort of Star-Trekian confederation of planets that offers advice to a variety of channelers all over the planet on what might be loosely defined as New Age topics like nuclear proliferation, ecological matters, spiritual values, holistic wellness, life after death, reincarnation and cosmic brotherhood. Ashtar, who is the head of this confederation made up of representatives from many different planets and realms, is said to be among the most highly advanced beings, one who is all but equal to the messiah (some have even declared him Jesus sent here over two thousand years ago on a spaceship).

And, to a degree, I would have to agree with Carol, We have perhaps dismissed this universal wisdom in favor of issuing warnings that not all of those who are arriving here through one method or another are our allies in doing battle against the forces of darkness.

Some, indeed, have come to plunder our planet and take advantage of its inhabitants, but there is still hope – if we are to accept the potentially valuable offerings coming to us from what would appear to be a group of highly evolved souls who would like to see us progress up the cosmic ladder to a heightened state of awareness.

This book is therefore about Ashtar, his council, their transmissions, and how examining and understanding the content of what they have to say could perhaps one day usher in a "thousand years" of global peace and harmony, which would allow us finally to take our rightful seat at the Free Federation of Planets.

Can Ashtar and his representatives – some of whom are living on Earth now – usher us into a Golden Age, a prosperous utopia for one and all? In the end, the reader must be the judge and jury of this controversial and divisive material. Turn the pages and reach forward to the stars!

## Timothy G. Beckley

mrufo8@hotmail.com

**A young Timothy Green Beckley contemplates a painting of Orthon, a Space Brother from Venus.**

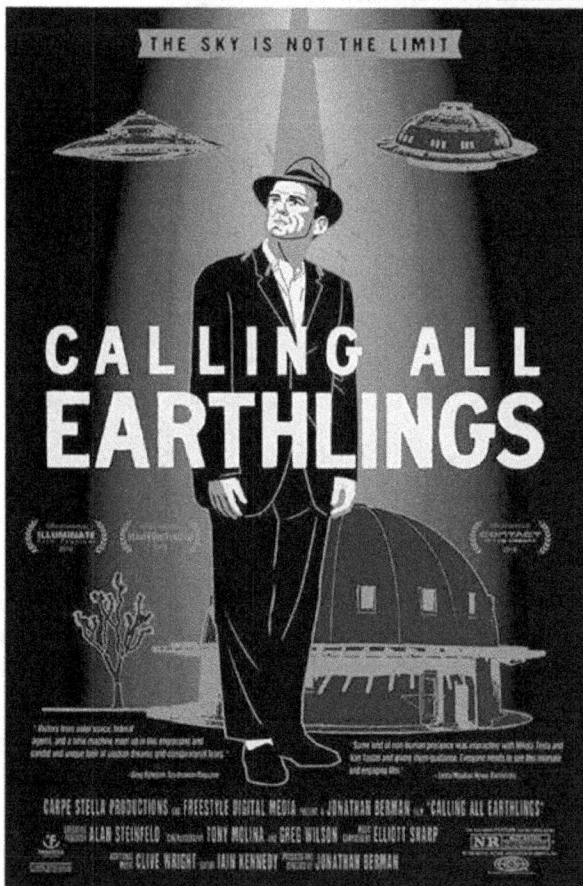

Above: An Ashtar Command representative, perhaps Solgonda, gave Van Tassel mental blueprints for a sort of "time machine," which he dubbed The Integratron. Van Tassel is shown with model here. www.integratron.com/history-about/

Left: If you're in the mood for a movie about George Van Tassel go to Amazon Prime or I Tunes and search for *Calling All Earthlings.*

# OUTER SPACE CHANNELERS - FROM ANCIENT ASTRONAUTS TO ASHTAR

## By Sean Casteel

The notion of receiving "channeled" messages from friendly extraterrestrials may be said to have begun in the mid-20th century, but the "New Age-y" phenomenon is really nothing new. The story of benevolent voices from beyond the vastness of time and space goes back well into ancient times, perhaps even as far back as the Bible.

In an interview conducted with publisher and writer Timothy Green Beckley, he made the effort to define just what a channel is.

"We think of channeling today," Beckley said, "in terms of speaking with higher entities, higher forms of intelligence, like Space People and beings from Atlantis. But it's hard to define really what a channeler is. Even Moses, maybe he channeled God, right?"

Beckley offered the Oracle of Delphi as perhaps the first channeler who used the same modus operandi as more modern practitioners of the art. The Oracle was a woman, or a succession of women, who claimed to be in contact with Zeus and some of the other members of the Greek pantheon.

"A lot of people today," Beckley said, "believe that there is a connection between the Greek and Roman gods and the Ancient Astronauts. They could have been one and the same."

It was at this location that the Oracle of Delphi received her channeled messages.
(Photo by Tim Beckley)

11

Beckley visited the site in Greece where the Oracle of Delphi gave her readings and wrote an account of the visit for "*FATE* Magazine" in 2006. This theory is perhaps best brought forward by one of this book's many fine contributors, in the embodiment of Hercules Invictus, who points out quite courageously the similarities between the old and the new contacts from what can only be described as the "beautiful space gods," be they extraterrestrial, interdimensional or inhabitants of a city beneath Mount Olympus.

"The oracle of Delphi was a channeler in her own right, but did not predict the future herself," Hercules writes. "She passed on the information she received while in a trance to one of the high priests who presided over the gathering, which attracted the high and mighty of Greek society as well as lower class members. To most, the oracle seemed to be speaking in indecipherable riddles. She usually began her discourse with utterings such as: 'I know the number of the sand. I know the measure of the sea.'

"And then she would improvise from there," Beckley does not hesitate to go on, "often speaking in unknown tongues only her priestly handlers could comprehend. Crowds would gather to ask questions, and they were most likely to receive a Yes or No answer. Frequently associated with the oracle's ability to foresee events was a mysterious vapor, which critics say rose from the cracks in the floor of the cubicle where the visionary would be seated on a tripod-like brass stool. The Christians propagated the idea that the prophetess was intoxicated by the fumes in order to step across the border into the void of the next world. They saw the oracle as a tool of the devil, much as fundamentalists today believe spirits are all Satan's conjurations used to fool people into believing there is no life beyond the pale."

Even Alexander the Great is said to have consulted the Oracle of Delphi, seeking information about his future military conquests. For the common person not embroiled in the machinations of war and politics, the oracle was available to answer personal questions. A query like "How do I cure my son of lovesickness?" would receive a therapeutic, albeit vague, response like "Treat him gently."

To paraphrase Heraclitus, the Greek philosopher, "The oracle neither conceals nor reveals the truth . . . only hints at it."

## JOHN DEE AND THE QUEEN

Another important link in the historical chain of channeling is John Dee, a Welsh mathematician who lived in the 16th and 17th centuries. He was also an astronomer and an occultist, whose reputation as a scholar was such that he sometimes served as a consultant to Queen Elizabeth I. Dee was a devoted student of alchemy, divination and Hermetic philosophy. He devoted much of his last thirty years to attempting to commune with angels in order to learn the universal language of creation and unify mankind prior to the coming apocalypse.

"He claimed to have spoken with angels," Beckley said, "and devised an entire mathematical occult code so that others could do so as well. This was at a time when witches and occultists were still being persecuted. Dee's work was supposed to be superior to anyone else's. Apparently, he made some predictions and some of them were very successful. So he was channeling angelic beings."

It should be noted that even though Dee is identified with the word "occultist," he was an extremely pious Christian who prayed and fasted as part of his preparations to attempt angelic contact. He did not draw a distinction between his mathematical research and his delving into angel summoning and divination. He considered the various efforts to be part of the same quest to find a transcendent understanding of the divine forms which underlie the visible world.

There are some among the many Ashtar channelers worldwide who proclaim that the mighty "spaceman" is, himself, an angel, and that the angels of the Bible might have actually been inhabitants of some far distant world. Rev. Barry Downing has perhaps, best of all, written on this topic in his *Biblical UFO Revelations* book also published, if you hadn't already guessed, by Inner Light – Global Communications.

## ALEISTER CROWLEY AND THE MYSTERIES HE CONJURED

Moving ahead a few centuries, Beckley also considers the widely influential occultist Aleister Crowley to be a significant channel, though his messages were most definitely not positive as are the ones from Ashtar and associates. Crowley was an avowed bisexual, a recreational drug experimenter and a social critic who claimed to be in a revolt against the moral and religious values of his time, the early 20th century. His cardinal rule was "Do What Thou Wilt," all of which led to a great deal of negative notoriety.

But Crowley has gotten a bad rap, perhaps deservingly, according to Beckley.

"Now, this is quite an interesting thing," Beckley continued. "Crowley believed there were other dimensions, other realities, and that there were beings that populated these other dimensions. A lot of people think of him as calling up demons, but that's not necessarily the case. Almost anything, if you're a certain kind of skeptic, can seem evil – just like some Christians think that every UFO being is a demon."

## A DWELLER ON TWO PLANETS

One often overlooked channeled work is a book called "*A Dweller On Two Planets*." The book was written by Frederick S. Oliver, who was born in 1866. He completed the manuscript in 1886, but it was not published until 1905, by Oliver's mother Mary, six years after the author's death.

In his preface to "*A Dweller On Two Planets*," Oliver claims the book was channeled through him by automatic writing, visions and mental "dictations" by a spirit calling himself "Phylos the Tibetan," who revealed the story to Oliver over a period of three years, starting in 1883. The first section is a complex first person account by Phylos of the culture of Atlantis, which had reached a high level of technological and scientific advancement. It includes a detailed history of the social, economic, political and religious forces shaping Atlantis, and relates how daily life in Atlantis featured inventions like antigravity air and submarine craft, television, wireless telephones, air conditioners and high speed rail. Obviously, some of these devices have become reality. Throughout the book, there are images of what are clearly cigar-shaped vehicles drawn while the channeler was in a trance. These illustrations look almost identical to the tubular space ships George Adamski purports to have observed through his telescope. Did Adamski "borrow the idea" for this book, or are his photos perhaps more authentic than one is willing at first to believe?

The book also deals with esoteric subjects like karma and reincarnation. In the book's second section, Phylos is reincarnated in 19th century America and must let his karma from Atlantis play itself out, both in terms of rewards and punishments.

"This book has probably influenced more people or led more people," Beckley commented, "to an understanding of the realm of channeling. I understand Shirley MacLaine was in a bookstore in Paris one day when the book literally fell into her hands. She was so impressed by it that she began her study of metaphysics and ended up, of course, writing the popular bestseller '*Out On A Limb*.'"

Beckley said his publishing company has put out – admittedly with my editorial skills – a modernized, updated version of "*A Dweller On Two Planets*" to make it more accessible  for present day readers.

Drawings in "*A Dweller On Two Planets*" look remarkably similar to objects photographed by famous UFO contactee George Adamski.

We have an edition," Beckley said, "that is totally new and easier to read and perhaps will resonate with a whole new generation. So that was one of the channeled books of the last 150 years or so that has had a great appeal. In fact, I remember I was selling copies of it when I started out as a bookseller in my middle teens. There are several editions that have been printed, but I think ours is the most comprehensible and the easiest for people to understand."

## A NEW BIBLE IS CHANNELED

Another spiritual classic Beckley has reprinted is called "*OAHSPE: A New Bible*." The book was first published in 1882 and was purportedly channeled from angelic sources who spoke in the name of Jehovah. The human contact was an American dentist named John Ballou Newbrough, who reported receiving the manuscript through automatic writing.

"Newbrough would arise every morning," Beckley said, "just before dawn, and would sit by candlelight at his typewriter, one of the first typewriters, and type at over 100 words a minute these spiritual messages from other realms. The book covers the history of the planet Earth and its inhabitants for the past 24,000 years, starting out on the continent of Pan that was supposed to be in the Pacific. This is a tremendous volume, and people have studied it for years. There are still groups around the country who gather to study and discuss '*OAHSPE*.' Believers in the revelations offered in the book are called 'Faithists.'"

## OAHSPE – 24,000 YEARS OF THE EARTH'S PAST REVEALED

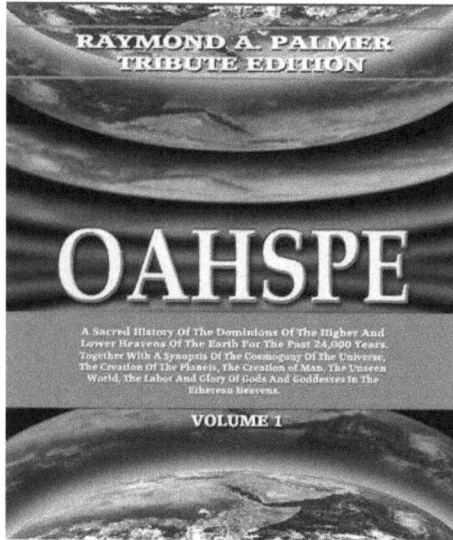

Coming in at approximately 1200 pages, our edition of "*Oahspe*" is the Ramond A. Palmer edition available as a two volume set from Amazon. Our edition has been edited and modernized.

Beckley's edition of the book is in two volumes that total over a thousand pages. He calls it "The Raymond Palmer Tribute Edition," owing to the fact that paranormal journalism pioneer Raymond Palmer promoted and sold the book in the mid-20th century. Well-known UFO researcher Wendell Stevens proclaimed "*OAHSPE*" to be the most important book of its type.

"*OAHSPE*" is a book of history, ethics and religion that emphasizes service to others as a basic component of how people's souls will one day be judged. It also describes a complex afterlife into which people pass on the way to becoming angels and occupants of heaven. Selfish behavior, base thoughts, or a non-vegetarian diet will land one in the lowest levels of heaven, while those who are simply evil must go to a kind of hell. But the ascension of everyone to a delightful mode of existence happens eventually in a place ruled by God. In the theology of "*OAHSPE*," God is an advanced angel ordained into office for a season, making it an honorary title held for a limited period of time.

While Beckley acknowledges that there were many books written on channeling in the decades after "*OAHSPE*" was first published, channeling actually came to its peak in a modern day sense in the early 1950s and 1960s, when many contactees began to claim that they communicated with extraterrestrials.

"Some of them had physical contact," Beckley said, "but a lot of them claimed to be channeling, that their bodies were actually 'taken over,' or their spirits were 'taken over' by these alien entities."

## VOICE OF THE ASHTAR COMMAND

The best known of these alien entities is called "Ashtar," the head of the Ashtar Command, said to be circling the Earth in a giant mother-ship above the equator. Many individuals all over the planet, not just here in the United States but also in Italy and England and other places, believe they have channeled Ashtar.

"His voice has been picked up on ham radio sets," Beckley said, "and a TV station in England was reportedly taken over and a transmission was made, supposedly by Ashtar. This was in the news in the 1970s. It was a well-known case, and a recording of it is out there on the Internet where you can actually hear the transmission."

www.youtube.com/watch?v=afXKOt3Aoxc

The first channeler of Ashtar, Beckley believes, was George Van Tassel.

"We think of George Van Tassel," Beckley explained, "as the fellow who ran the very successful UFO conferences and conventions in Joshua Tree, California, out there at Giant Rock, right in the middle of the desert. Every October for at least ten years, thousands of people would gather on his property. He rented it from the federal government. He had an airstrip where people would fly in and a little restaurant. People from all over the world would come every October to hear the words of the contactees.

"George had a big platform that was erected next to Giant Rock," Beckley continued, "and people would ascend the stairs and tell their stories. Some of the individuals would have been Daniel Fry, Orfeo Angelucci, George Adamski, and Howard Menger. It was quite an attraction. Even *'Look Magazine'* did a big pictorial on it at one point."

The first channeled messages from the Ashtar Command are said to have issued forth through George Van Tassel as he sat in a room dug under Giant Rock Airport, just outside of Landers, California, in the desert. Here the late, iconic, all night radio talk show host Long John Nebel speaks with George.

Giant Rock itself was at one time the largest standing boulder in North America, until it was split apart by an earthquake a few years ago. A room had been dug out directly under the rock where George Van Tassel and his family would gather on a regular basis. Van Tassel would go into a trancelike state and receive messages from Ashtar and other entities.

George Hunt Williamson, who had been a witness to George Adamski's sightings in the California desert that included a face-to-face meeting with a blonde-haired Venusian, also channeled in that same period in the early 1950s.

"People were very impressed by this," Beckley said. "Sometimes the entities being channeled would make predictions, like where they would appear in the sky on such and such a date. People would gather and have sightings of these craft. In fact, an admiral from the US Navy set up a channeling session one time and the same thing happened. He had a woman that he knew was channeling entities from space and they had a sighting based upon her prediction. This is even in the Project Blue Book report, and we did a whole chapter on it in our book '**Round Trip To Hell In A Flying Saucer**.'

"So there's really nothing new about channeling, but it is still very popular. Shirley MacLaine and various other metaphysical writers have made it even more popular in recent years."

## THE PRIMARY REPRESENTATIVE FOR ASHTAR APPEARS

According to Beckley, the main representative on Earth of the Ashtar Command was an elderly woman named Thelma Turrell, who later changed her name to Tuella on the recommendation of the space entities she was communicating with. Throughout the book we hear from her more than any other source for this information, as Beckley believes she is one of the original, "and more credible," voices speaking as a representative of the Command.

"She was born here on this planet," Beckley said, "but spiritual entities took over her body. She was one of these individuals we've identified as 'Walk-Ins.' She channeled Ashtar on a regular basis."

Before her passing, channeler Tuella was the primary representative of the Ashtar Command.

The tone or attitude of Tuella's voice did not change when she was in contact with Ashtar, as if she was in an altered "channeling" state of being; she seemed to be speaking normally. Her sessions with Ashtar were recorded and transcribed and eventually became part of a series of books published originally by Guardian Actions Publications. Beckley's publishing company, Global Communications/Inner Light Books, bought the rights to Tuella's books just before she passed away. The titles include "**Ashtar, A Tribute, Revealing His Secret Identity**," "**Project World Evacuation**," "**On Earth Assignment**," "**Master Symbol of the Solar Cross**," and most recently, "**A New Book of Revelation**."

"She had people who came from all over the United States," Beckley said, "to see her and talk to her and to receive these channeled messages. She's very, very popular and highly respected even today for being the primary channel for the Ashtar Command. She got into some political things, but her message was always about peace, love and harmony."

Ashtar, the inspiration for much of that peace, love and harmony, of course remains a rather enigmatic figure about who little is known. In one of the reprints reissued by Beckley and Inner Light Books, called "**Ashtar, A Tribute, Revealing His Secret Identity**," a chapter called "Who Is Ashtar?" grapples with this problem. It is said that Ashtar is the Christian Commander from Venus, and that he ranks just below an entity called Jesus-Sananda in overseeing the Airborne Division of the Brotherhood of Light.

"His messages are beamed from a colossal Starship or Space Station," the chapter continues, "beyond our atmosphere. He is loved for his deeply philosophical approach to our global problems and his efforts to raise planetary vibrations. Ashtar speaks of twenty million extraterrestrial persons involved with his Command in the Program For Planet Earth, and of another four million on our physical plane, consciously or unconsciously cooperating in the Program of Light."

Ashtar is a devoted Christian who declares the "Christ Teacher of this Galaxy" to be his beloved Commander-In-Chief, saying that Christ's Word is the law Ashtar himself obeys to fulfill the Program of Light on Earth.

The book also includes a Q. and A. with Ashtar conducted by a believer named Trevor James in 1958 in which Ashtar says that his body is etheric and that he possesses no physical "casing" of the dense type that humans are limited to. He is also called a Herald Angel by other trance mediums who claim contact with him.

Further along in the "Ashtar" book, Tuella receives "A Message of Encouragement From Ashtar."

"We come to you in the vibration of Love and Light," Ashtar begins, "sent forth from the Upper Heavens to penetrate the atmosphere of Earth and reach the hearts of all Mankind. We enfold the Planet with the power of Love and blend into its very layers an anointing of peace and goodwill. We carry away the off cast thoughts of darkness that would destroy your world if left unchecked. We intervene with our own magnetic rays and beams of Greater Light to keep the balance for further decades. White light is enfolded around and around your world in an essence of purification that will bring the blessings of God upon all Nations.

"Wherever there is a hostile approach to the solution of world problems, our Greater Light will assist to dissolve that hostility and maintain peace. Factions of baser intent are gradually deteriorating and being replaced by understanding and goodwill. Peace will come, and the lesser infiltrations of the Dark Ones will be overcome. Yield not to weariness of spirit, but continue to watch for our coming, and the fulfillment of all the dreams and hopes of Humanity for a better world. It will come. The waters of Life shall flow upon every barren place, and every thirst shall be quenched."

Sounds encouraging indeed. Which of course is the whole point, says Beckley.

"We think of alien abductions as very negative things," Beckley said. "People like Travis Walton and Whitley Strieber being taken onboard UFOs and being physically harassed and examined and perhaps even raped. While the channeled messages are just the opposite. They deal with bliss and euphoria and they talk about a better world and how we can live a better life.

"They take a higher spiritual tone," he went on, "than a lot of the other contacts and experiences. People always ridicule this and say it's a lot of New Age fluff. And they're right. A lot of the things the channelers say cannot really be verified. But it's a very positive message that they bring, although of course it's hard for many people to follow or believe in in this chaotic world that we live in."

While Beckley is of course correct that the inspiring messages from Ashtar to Tuella and the other channelers cannot be documented or proven, one cannot help but wish it is true somehow that someone out there really cares about us and is watching over us. Perhaps the Ashtar Command is really the modern day version of our planet's ancient guardian angels beliefs given a more technological spin? We can only hope.

## RECOMMENDED READING

*ASHTAR: REVEALING THE SECRET IDENTITY OF THE FORCES OF LIGHT AND THEIR SPIRITUAL PROGRAM FOR EARTH.*

*A NEW BOOK OF REVELATION – A HARVESTING OF SOULS AT EARTH'S FINAL MOMENT*

*PROJECT WORLD EVACUATION: UFOS TO ASSIST IN THE "GREAT EXODUS" OF HUMAN SOULS OFF THIS PLANET*

*MASTER SYMBOL OF THE SOLAR CROSS*

- Other books, such as "**On Earth Assignment**" and "**Cosmic Prophecies**," can also be located. Just make sure it is a reputable edition of Inner Light – Global Communications, as it has been edited according to her wishes.

No matter what the situation, it is claimed that Ashtar has, and can, help the world out.

**Ashtar: New Rendition By Carol Ann Rodriguez**

# A CONVERSATION WITH TUELLA
## By Timothy Green Beckley

This purports to be the only existing picture taken of Commander Ashtar while in materialized mode.

**H**is words have been received by many the world over. And while no one has ever seen him in a physical sense (debatable?), few can deny that he speaks with a power and a majesty that heralds great wisdom and knowledge that could only have been obtained through centuries of deep study and enlightenment. There are those who steadfastly maintain that Ashtar is about the wisest space being assigned to our solar system, a dedicated and highly advanced soul who has reincarnated many times to the point where he can now truly be considered a Master in the same category as Jesus, Buddha and other avatars. Fact is some believe he is the Christ who came to our world on a space voyage, with the idea in mind of changing the world. In short, he is the Messenger of the New Age, assigned to the task of bringing Earth safely through the troubled times that will most certainly cross our path in the next few years.

One earthly channel who wishes to identify himself only by the initials E.P.H. has received many messages from Ashtar through automatic writing, as well as while in an altered state of consciousness. This channel makes the point that throughout both psychic phenomena and the Bible, "there are orders of beings, called by various names, who in times of great need, especially, come to earth to offer their assistance to men. Why shouldn't they be able to impress thoughts and ideas on receptive individuals?" E.P.H. justly wants to know. "After all," the channel reminds us, "down through the ages there have been mystics who claimed they have heard the voice of God or of angels. Today, there are those who claim to hear the voice of spacemen. And if flying saucers are real, why shouldn't they be manned by intelligent beings who can send their thought-waves to those who are receptive?" It would appear that Ashtar has been doing exactly what E.P.H. suggests, and the scope of his influence is expanding as more and more sensitive individuals are picking up on his words of encouragement.

## GUARDIAN ACTION

Among those who claim to have channeled Ashtar is — as we will often be reminded — the late Thelma Terrell head of Guardian Action International, and an acknowledged New Age leader during her life. Thelma says her calling as a spiritual messenger began in the early Seventies, with her channeling work starting in 1979, when she was commissioned by the Ashtar Command to use the spiritual name of "Tuella." Before turning her work over to this publishing company upon realizing that she would have to return due to exceedingly ill health, Tuella published numerous channeled works, including "World Messages For The Coming Decade," a cosmic symposium of some 27 speakers (including nine noted Space Commanders and representatives of the Satumium Council, as well as "Ashtar, A Tribute" and the very popular book *Project World Evacuation.*" (*When ordering please be certain it is the authorized Inner Light – Global Communications edition you are sending for.*)

## NATIONAL DISASTERS ON THE RISE

In transmissions which she has received via mental telepathy from the Ashtar Command, this highly evolved intelligence says that news of disasters will soon reach a magnitude that the news media will be at a loss to report them all. "Television reports will fill the day in continuing attempts to cover these events, so recurrent will be the disasters, so widespread the locations. These have been referred to as changes that must come. The restlessness of the inner earth which awakens the sleeping volcanoes to belch forth their living fire, is the same momentum which manifests elsewhere as tremors or earthquakes of small or large magnitude. Tidal waves and intense weather abnormalities; shifting plates of land beneath the oceans and the quivering of the mountains, could take  place in concerted action, so that humanity would have nowhere to run, nowhere to turn and no sense of direction or idea of what they must do to save themselves. Panic could grip the hearts of people resulting in calls upon God for deliverance. It is in hours such as these THAT YOUR SKIES WILL FILL WITH THE SHIPS OF YOUR BROTHERS FROM OTHER REALMS."

At this time such messages were received the term "climate change" was not in use, and certainly it appears these transmissions from other realms hit the nail on the head with their prediction of catastropic global weather patterns.

One of the things that the Ashtar Command has requested at this point in time is that they be allowed to come forward and be permitted to take a place in the international body as well as in our own Congress. I remember the Earl of Clancarty telling me upon my speaking at the House of Lords in the UK that they would like at least two alien representatives to appear in chamber, and deliver a full on message to the British governing body. I guess I had to take on this position as I did speak about Ashtar when addressing the closed chamber committee. An alien I am not. Lol!

Said Ashtar: "We extend to your President, the House of Representatives, the men of the Senate and all of the national leaders, our hand of friendship and cooperation. In the name of the salvation of the life of Humanity, we ask that you would receive our words and welcome us to speak in your assemblies. We have those who can walk among you and never be noticed for all their similarity to your own appearance. They can suddenly appear behind your rostrum and speak to the members of your Congress. We would prefer to be invited to do this. If we are not invited to do this we may have to arrange our own opportunity, to speak to these gentlemen, in the early part of this decade. For there is too much at stake on an interplanetary basis to stand by without an effort to probe the motivations behind present world disorder. We send this message as an advancing envoy and ask the world leaders and the governments of all the world to make a place for our spokesmen upon your agendas."

Ashtar's closing words on this matter is quite clear: "IF THE SPACE IS MADE THE SPOKESMAN WILL APPEAR!"

Could it be that eventually our world leaders will have to start listening to these highly evolved beings, regardless of whether they want to or not? Recently, the President said he was briefed on some of the previously classified reports involving military pilots, a story of which appeared first in the New York Times, but spread rapidly throughout the news media.

In Reno, Nevada, many years ago, I had the honor to share the same speakers platform with Tuella and during a brief break in the proceedings managed to sneak in a casual interview with this remarkable New Age lady whose channeling abilities reaped her a host of dedicated students from coast to coast. Here is what Tuella had to tell me about Ashtar, her vision of a predicted world evacuation, and the overall plan of our brothers and sisters from the depths of space. It was obviously that she was no holding back with her religious views mixing a bit of Golden Age Christianity with the philosophy of the space people. Not my kick, but I never want to put words in a person's mouth or change the meaning of what they have to say.

**Beckley**: You are one of the many channels who are in regular contact with Ashtar and his command. What sort of messages are now coming through?

**Teulla**: Most of the recent channeling has to do with a mass evacuation off this globe before a disaster strikes. My book PROJECT: WORLD EVACUATION was meant to help get people ready and to know what to expect. In this way much of the trauma is removed should that event become necessary.

**Beckley**: How did you first start channeling, what is your background in this field, and what were you doing before you got involved in all this?

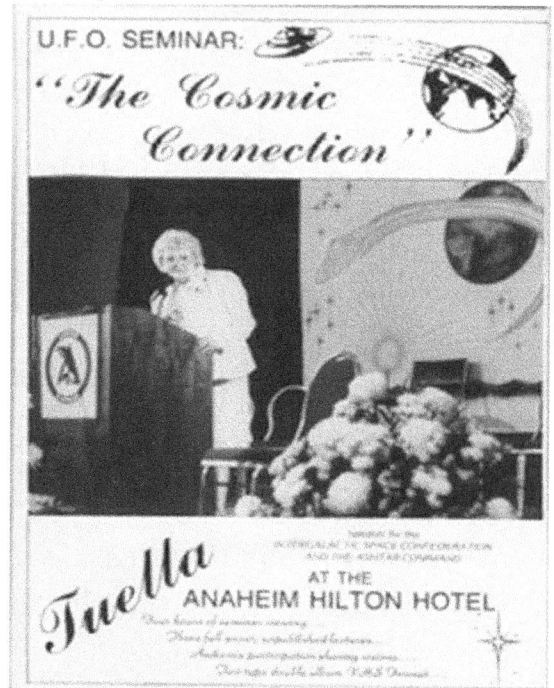

**Tuella**: I was a servant of Jesus Christ long before I knew anything about this. I was a pastor, an evangelist and I was a lover of the scriptures. My first unusual experience came when I'd be seeking scriptures for my sermons. Someone would be standing behind me discussing certain passages. It began in that fashion - someone hovering over me and teaching me. Then, finally the things I was taught far exceeded the creed to which I was bound. Soon, I moved out and the teachings expanded. That is how I found a closer relationship with my own spiritual teachers.

**Beckley**: For those not so familiar with this sort of thing, could you tell us something about Ashtar, and the Ashtar Command, and those that make up his group?

**Tuella**: Ashtar himself is a very beautiful being. He is from the Venus heritage line. There are six planets up there, there is Venus, and Astara, Volga, and Ashtar, and Eros, and that group of planets. He is from that line, but he is the Commander in Chief of this hemisphere, for all the fleets that are coming in from all of the other planets and galaxies. We have other commanders who are in charge of other hemispheres. Ashtar has been called the Christian Commander and he is very close to the Lord Jesus Christ. Of course, Jesus is referred to as our great beloved Commander. The next in authority over Ashtar is Jesus Sananda Himself. All that takes place within the atmosphere of the earth is the responsibility of the space federation which is under the direct jurisdiction of Ashtar himself.

**Beckley**: You are a space channel. You do receive messages from Ashtar and from those under his command. Have you ever seen Ashtar materialize? Have you seen him in the physical sense, and could you describe him?

**Tuella**: He does not materialize. These fellows from this level of evolution do not materialize. What they do is send a projection of themselves to you, so that rather than seeing, you perceive. If you are sensitive, you sense what they look like and what they are wearing.

In the opening pages of my book, I do get into a description of what is was like when Ashtar appeared to me and I use the term "appear" loosely. When he appears, it is a projection that he sends, mind to mind, just as he sends his words mind to mind. It is truly a function of telepathy.

**Beckley**: How many messages have you channeled to date?

**Tuella**: I have no idea there have been so many. I still have in my files pretty much everything I have ever received. I have 12 years of training with them.

One of the beings very prominent in my training is a being called Athena. I did not know at the time anything about the Space Con-federation, but I found out later that Athena is the twin flame of Ashtar. He has said to me that he could turn over the whole command to her and no one would even miss him. She is that efficient in her job. She is the one who had taken over my training for many years. It was not until 1980 that Ashtar came in and asked me to take over a certain chore, and began to communicate with me in a direct way. But, even now, he does not come in unless it is something of great importance. Usually, one of the other commanders or someone else comes in.

**Beckley**: What, at this moment, would you say is their most important function?

**Tuella**: The most important thing right now is that they want the world to know why they are here. They want fear removed so it will not hinder what they are trying to do. And they want the world to know that there is a very, very strong possibility that events may make a world evacuation necessary before much longer.

They have indicated that there probably will be great geological changes, not necessarily war. They do not intend to let nuclear war go on for any length of time. But, nuclear war may precipitate severe geological events.

**Beckley**: How many people have they chosen for this evacuation and how have they been chosen?

**Tuella**: They do not choose people for this evacuation. The people have already made their choices long ago. Therefore, they qualify by virtue of the lives they have lived and by the frequency of their own electromagnetic field or their aura as it is called. If they had their way they would take everyone and everyone would go. Everyone will receive an invitation, but not everyone can endure the frequencies of the levitation beams.

Ashtar greeting his far flung fellow Federation members.

**Ashtar Command and the Galactic Federation of Light are an alliance of spiritual and extraterrestrial beings that seek to bring humanity into a higher level of existence.**

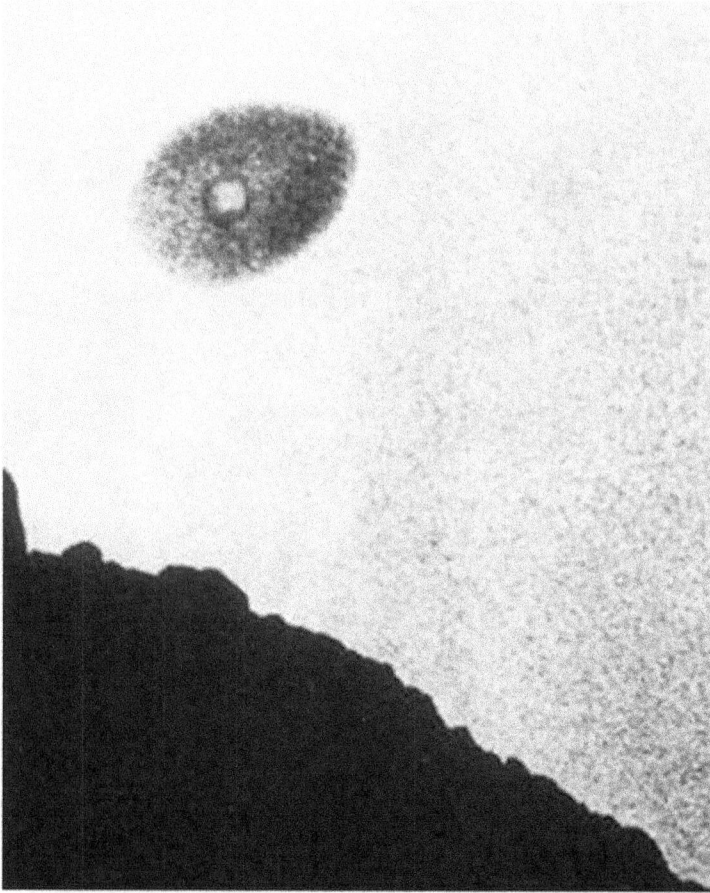

Using infrared film, Trevor James Constable photographed strange objects in the sky that couldn't be seen with the naked eye.

Constable theorized that UFOs came from a parallel universe known as "Etheria" and that there were two categories of UFO, some were machines and others living creatures.

Could these objects be Etheric beings or their spaceships?

# ARE WE ETHERIANS?

**I** think it's necessary to understand the physical characteristics of Ashtar – is he truly physical or more of a spirit dweller? His existence has been interpreted in both ways. This is a discussion that Tuella passed along to help with our understanding of the situation. This interview places the "spacemen" in the ethereal category.

• • • • • •

Trevor James Constable discovered a wholly invisible world of the etheric.

*In 1958, Trevor James released "**They Live in the Sky**," published by Dr. Franklin Thomas through New Age Publishing Company. The book contained several fascinating and informative interviews with Ashtar. Mr. James poses direct questions to the Commander:*

**Question**: Are you Etheric beings? Or are you possessed of a fleshly physical body such as mine?

**Ashtar**: I am Etheric. I do not have a fleshly body like yours, bounded by flesh. But it is possible for me to make my being visible to your optics by certain changes in its vibratory rate.

**Question**: This would mean, then, that you are normally invisible to us?

**Ashtar**: Yes.

If we take Ashtar at his word, we have explanations for some of the alleged encounters with space beings, and also for the fact that both ships and controlling intelligences are known to be invisible on occasions. These beings can convert to a vibratory rate where they are visible to us, but normally belong in a higher vibration.

**Question:** As you are an Etheric being, are other Etheric beings visible to you?

**Ashtar:** Yes, although not exactly in terms of optical vision as you know it.

It was about eighteen months after this communication had been received that I gained a rather startling proof of its validity. I paid a call on a distinguished European lady in Los Angeles with an international reputation as a seer and psychic. Discussing various aspects of her faculty with me and answering my questions, she suddenly sat bolt upright in her chair. "Have you ever had any contact with any non-physical beings?" she asked, with a smile. I replied that I believed that I had, but could not be completely sure.

She then said, "There is a magnificent-looking being standing beside you, and he communicates to me that is name is Ashtar. Do you know him?" I replied that the personality was familiar, and she gave me a full description of him as she saw him clairvoyantly. Seven feet or so tall, extremely stern, helmeted, and giving the impression of being a sort of a military man.

This was extremely interesting insofar as Ashtar had described himself as the "Commandant, Vela Quadra Sector, Realms of Schare, All Projections, All Waves," and therefore would probably be a military type of being.

In possession of just the beginnings of these general theories, I addressed further questions to Ashtar on this subject.

**Question:** From your statement that you are Etheric, am I to presume that you have evolved beyond the stage of a Physical and Astral body?

**Ashtar:** Correct. I do not possess a physical casing of the dense type such as yours. I am definitely Etheric, as are the people on other Planets in this Solar System. However, this does not mean that we are invisible to each other as we are to you under normal circumstances. We see each other and live much as you do, but we do not have this dense physical casing which you possess. The advantages, benefits and comforts of this living are enormous, and the irritations of the fleshly envelope are most uncomfortable. Unless we choose to convert the vibrational frequency of our bodies to one which is visible to your optics, we remain invisible to your people. Highly evolved people, with a good 'psychic eye,' as you call it, can sometimes see us in vaporous form, although we may be invisible to other Earthlings in the same location. When your clairvoyants travel to our civilizations on other planets, they see and are able to interpret our lives because they are not using their physical eyes but their Astral or Psychic sight, to which we are visible just as though we were physical.

*Question:* When you become visible to our eyes, does the person who sees you know that you are a 'converted Etheric'?

*Ashtar:* Not as a rule. The conversion can be made so completely that a physical person encountering us thinks that we, too, are physical.

*Question:* What of those who claim to have been up in your craft?

*Ashtar:* In our contacts with Earthlings, we have to be careful not to go beyond their understanding. In these instances, the ships and all entities within them are converted to a vibrational level at which they had the substance of physical things as known to you. Whether the experience was Physical or Astral is not known to some people who had the experience.

*Question:* I wish to ask a question or two concerning Etheric substance.

*Ashtar:* We will be glad to answer whatever we can for you. We wish to arm you with as much knowledge as possible, and are limited in this only by your power to assimilate it. I do not wish to talk over your head, but we will supply you with knowledge to the limit of your understanding.

*Question:* I am puzzled by the concept of Etheric matter. For example, there is one case on record where one of our jet aircraft flew right through a space ship without hitting anything solid whatever. Are your ships made of a vaporous substance, or are they a different form of Earthly matter?

*Ashtar:* We have all the elements you know on Earth, and many more. The Etheric form of these metals differs in its atomic and molecular structure from Earth-made metals. For example, the distance between the nucleus and the orbiting electrons of the Etheric iron nucleus is much greater than in iron as you know it on Earth. This permits the atoms of Earthly steel to pass right through the atoms of Etheric steel in such a way nothing happens to either form of steel. The Etheric form of steel enjoys a higher vibratory rate than Earthly steel and therefore is not apparent to Earthly vision or, if you prefer, physical eyesight. Under certain circumstances it becomes visible, as in the presence of certain atmospheric gases of Shan (Earth) or at will in accordance with the desire of the controlling intelligence. No matter how great the mass of the Etheric substance, even a space ship measuring many miles across in your measure, physical matter cannot damage or injure it or its contents.

*Question*: When you speak of making Etheric matter visible at will, is this the way that George Adamski was permitted to take his now-famous photographs?

*Ashtar*: Yes. Ether ships, as they have been called on your surface, have been made visible to and for certain individuals, selected upon your surface, of whom Adamski is one. Normally, the ships are part of the invisible world.

*Question*: If one were to develop astral vision or the psychic eye, would he be able to see the ships?

*Ashtar*: No. Not unless the vibratory rate of the ship were converted to the vibratory range of astral vision. Remember, the Etheric vibratory rate is higher than the Astral. Very few physical humans have some perception of the Etheric, but they are not normal people as you know them and for the most part dwell in very secluded places. As a general rule, perception of the Etheric through vision cannot be accomplished except through the will of the Etheric, converting Etheric substance to a vibratory level where it is physically visible.

*Question*: In our Solar System, are there any other physical beings like us?

*Ashtar*: No. All beings on other planets in your Solar System are Etherics. On your planet, as you now know, there are two kinds of beings – Physical and Astral. Outside the Earth-Moon System in your Solar System, all are Etheric."

An Etherian ship photographed near Giant Rock. It was
only made visible by using infrared photography.

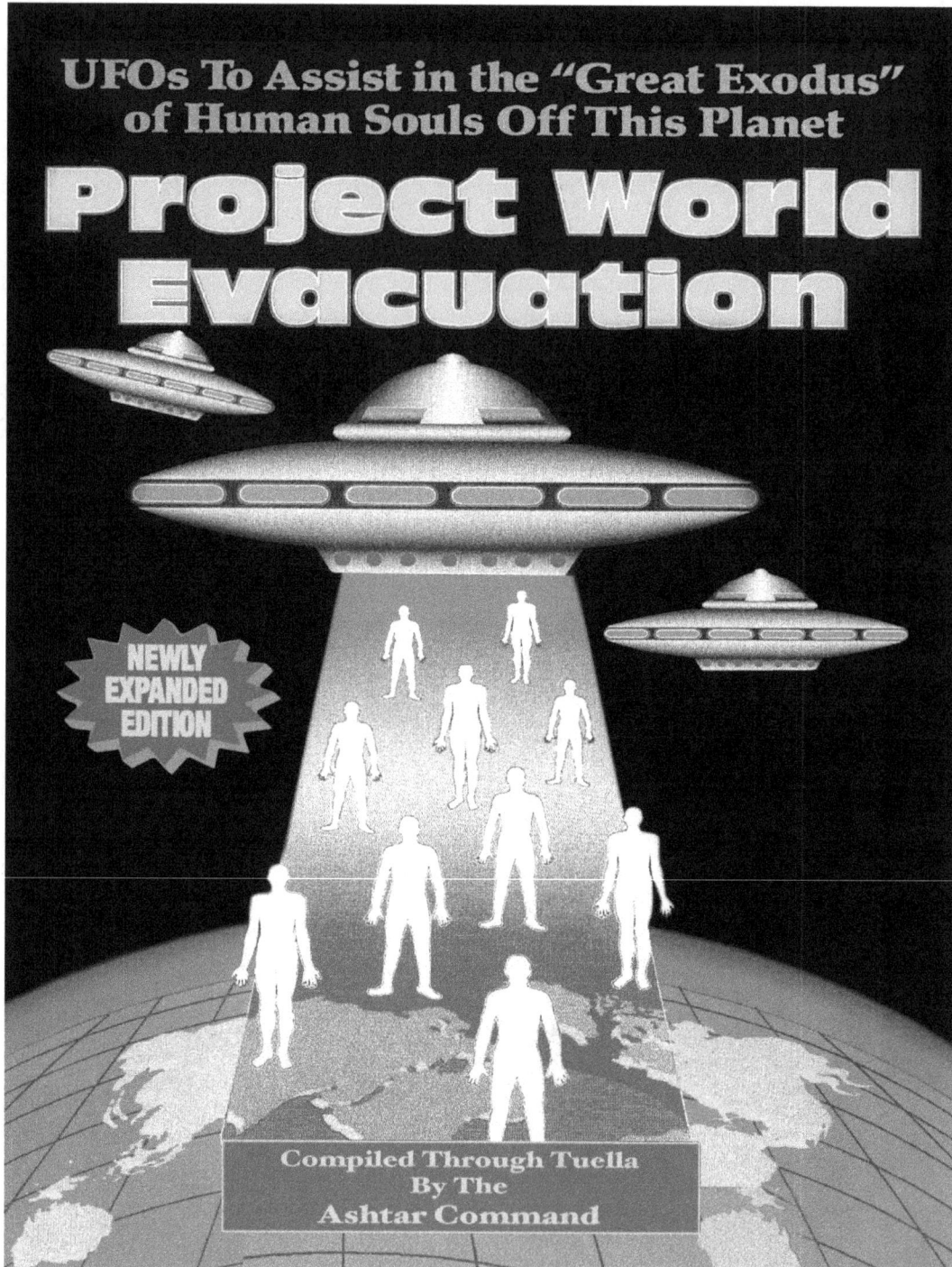

UFOs To Assist in the "Great Exodus" of Human Souls Off This Planet

# Project World Evacuation

NEWLY EXPANDED EDITION

Compiled Through Tuella
By The
Ashtar Command

Barbara Leeds came up with this version for *"Project World Evacuation"* when Inner Light took over the publication of the book after Tuella's transition.

## TALK OF AN EVACUATION – IS IT STILL TO COME?

In the late 1970s and early 80s, the population of Earth – or at least those who are cosmically aware – were told that in case of a global disaster the "chosen" would be removed to a safe harbor in space. Tuella went into great detail in the work produced for the Ashtar Command, *"Project World Evacuation,"* which was well received in the New Age community. It inspired many to get their lives in order and to "get packing," should the time arrive for a lift off.

We are told that this book was written with the specific intention of awakening the beings who have a mission to accomplish, and to make them aware of the help they can bring to their fellow men in this troubled period of humanity. It is well underlined by the ET that the elected representatives will receive all the necessary support to continue their work and the disclosure of the truth.

The messages come from about 20 Masters, Guides and Extraterrestrial Commanders, grouped under the name: THE ASHTAR COMMAND, and were originally published by Guardian Action Publications out of Durango, Colorado. The copyright, along with Tuella's other titles, was turned over to Timothy Green Beckley of Inner Light Publications upon her death as detailed in a contract that was drawn up.

Here's an appropriate excerpt from one Ashtar message:

"I am ASHTAR, the commander of millions of men who protect your land and form the alliance of peace in the INTERGALACTIC COUNCIL. We used Tuella, our messenger, to compile this book and to disclose to humans the details of a forthcoming Extra-Terrestrial intervention, for the Heavenly Father does nothing without first notifying His prophets.

British artist Pennington drafted the art for the first cover of "*Project World Evacuation.*"

"There is a method and good organization in our detailed plan with the specific purpose of removing the souls of this planet in the event of disaster requiring rescue. It is necessary to consider a tilting of the poles, a collision with an asteroid or any other danger caused by man himself.

"We want to expose our most secret strategy and sound the alarm to make you aware that we arrived at the fateful hour.

"We want to reveal to you and give you proofs of our presence, of our existence and especially of the protection that extends over you.

"We want to let you know that we remind our elect to spend a brief time with us in our spaceships before returning to Earth to help you, and to share with you the revelations that will prove our existence and the truthfulness of our words.

"This book is not dedicated to the masses, but to the few who can understand, so that later those who will be left out will know why they were not removed.

"Read and understand that the inner vibration of the Being, the Spiritual Man, must be accelerated."

Master Kouthoumi adds:

"The time is coming when these special emissaries will be temporarily removed from the Earth to receive from us a special instructive training and personal guidance to prepare them for their future tasks. It is necessary that these evolved beings receive our special attention in order to prepare them for their mission.

"There are many millions of these light-flooded universal volunteers dedicated totally to serving the Heavenly Government, the Solar Hierarchy and the Intergalactic Confederation in a total effort to save the planet.

"Because of the impending danger of divergent energies encircling the globe, the elect must prepare for an abduction and a change in their normal terrestrial life over a period of 14 to 21 days."

Andromeda Rex, another Extraterrestrial Commander, explains that those who will be abducted will have the chance to bring back material evidence of their stay in the light ships. The signs and wonders that will be given will remove all doubt and skepticism. These souls have been chosen and trained for a long time for this kind of work because the preparations for this program have already been put in place a hundred years ago.

These chosen beings, who are now working in the media, commerce, education, churches, etc., will meet and be related to each other in a common work to make known concretely through books, articles, texts and conferences the presence of the Extraterrestrial Beings.

This kidnapping and gathering will be done with the specific purpose of convincing humanity. Powerful forces will be given to those who can sustain the high vibrations to enable them to function at their ultimate capacity, and to their body of light to vibrate at the wavelengths of the Extraterrestrials, this in order to form a greater unity of intention among all the Forces of Light.

The work of synthesis must intensify. The conscious desire to be a conscious portion of a Whole must grow in us every day. This thought, often reaffirmed, will accelerate our vibrations and prepare us for the abduction.

In another message, ASHTAR tells us again: "These kidnappings will not all be undertaken simultaneously on the globe, but rather by sectors, or regions. There are seven kidnappings that are planned one after the other to contact and advise the elect of the earth. They will be sure to receive beforehand a signal and a very clear message, which will in no way be misinterpreted, warning them of their departure.

"We bring together all those who have spiritual work or who have a responsibility in this area. This gathering will be done in a conscious state. You will always keep your mindfulness at all times during your stay, and you can talk about it when you return. You will even receive two objects: two tangible proofs: an object that you will carry on you, and the other that you will hold in your hand. This experience and evidence will give you assured spiritual authority that will never be taken away from you. You will be anointed, and receive a certificate and spiritual gifts that will represent the authenticity of your initiation and mission. You will become the representatives of the Celestial Government and the Great Intergalactic Council.

"I greet all my brothers and sisters of Light with the sign of the Solar Cross. I give you my blessing knowing each one of you in particular. Be ready! Be alert! Be attentive to the call! I am ASHTAR who has the responsibility of millions of men, and who works for your beloved Commander-in-Chief, Jesus Christ, Savior of the world!"

## SUMMARY

Upcoming events in chronological order:

### Abduction of the Elected

This kidnapping and gathering will be temporary and short-lived and will aim to educate "leaders" to get them to know each other. This will not necessarily happen at the time of planetary disorders. The Elect will return to Earth for final removal later.

### Phase I

In times of severe crisis for the world and serious global disorders, Phase I evacuation will be triggered in seconds without notice. All Elect, teachers, teachers and spiritual leaders, as well as their followers, will be removed, except those of the "Special Legion," who will remain on Earth to help until the last minute. All these privileged Beings will be levitated and brought to the small vessels, which will then bring them to the great mothership, very high in the atmosphere. There will be no landing of ships for Phase I, as they will remain in the heavens.

### Phase II

The second phase of the global evacuation will take place for those who have tried to follow the Light Teachers, and who will have a sufficiently high spiritual vibration, and also for the children. These children will be accompanied by those who love them and are responsible for their safety. These young and these babies will be levitated in "suspended animation" to avoid any shock or trauma.

### Phase III

The third phase will take place to allow all those beings who will remain on Earth and who wish to join the Extraterrestrials, to be able to leave. The sky will be filled with spacecraft that will launch an invitation to those who will not be frightened and who can withstand a certain vibratory frequency.

Andromeda Rex tells us again:

"The Great Evacuation will come upon the world in a sudden way, like a flash that shines through the sky. It will be so fast that the event will be almost over before you become aware of it. And it will be so when the events that require this action will manifest on this planet.

"It is not possible to describe all the details of these events, but we can reassure you of our protection and our vigilance about you. Our spaceships will be able to get close enough to the Earth to activate our beams of light that will transport you and direct you into our ships. The frequency of these beams of light is higher than any terrestrial electrical vibration. Our messages throughout history have always been about changing your vibration and trying to bring it up. Moreover, all religions and spiritual messages have advocated selfless love. Only those who lived in harmony with the Will of the Father will have no problem to support the beam of evacuation rays!

"There is nothing for you to fear about being among us. On the contrary, you will feel at home in an atmosphere of friendship and good neighborliness, with a great desire to help the neighbor in difficulty. We have clothes for you, and food that you will enjoy, and you can rest assured that your needs will be met. We will be your friends, and you will be happy with us, especially when you see your planet in disarray and you will feel the happiness of having escaped the cataclysms.

"Those who have been levitated in their physical bodies will have their atoms accelerated into this body to attain a more spiritual essence and become what is called a Body of Light. The physical form will remain similar in appearance, but this intimate blend of etheric and physical will bring beneficial changes for you that will eliminate disease and physical disharmony.

"Your stay with us will be of sufficient duration to allow your land to be purified and refurbished, and will at the same time give you the time needed to learn the lessons and teachings of the New Age.

"Our high technology will be at your disposal and we will help you and guide you to use this 'Supra-Science.' Those who will not be ready to accept this phenomenal change in harmony with the vibrations of the Aquarian Age will be transported to other less evolved planets, more adapted to the old thought of the Age of the Pisces."

To finish the synthesis of this book, we give the floor to Master Hilarion, Emerald Ray:

"I come to you so that my words may be heard and diffused by all the servants of Light in the world at this moment of crisis for humanity.

"It is imperative that those who are connected in any way to the Spiritual Hierarchy make a tremendous effort to come closer to one another with more love and tolerance so that a greater unity of thought and intentions can bring blessings to the Children of Light. We see from our spheres too many divisions and a lack of cohesion in your businesses.

"I ask you to put aside any attitude of separateness, to unite yourself in an impenetrable wall of Light against the forces of darkness who only think to divide to better defeat you. Do not tolerate any interference from these forces and visualize a blue light around each group, each circle, each being stretched toward the Light. Even human imperfection cannot disturb your inner peace and your vision of an ideal world. Do not allow your personality to weaken your soul.

"We are at a time when the greatest love must prevail. Patience and love should inspire every joint endeavor and effort to strengthen our Hierarchical program. The times have come when LOVE must unite you in a reinforced concentration of pure and powerful thoughts. The gates of hell can do nothing against love in action concentrated in the heart of an enlightened being!

"May my blessing be on each of you who serve the Light."

**The evacuation of Planet Earth will come in a sudden way, like a flash that shines through the sky.**

Other artists have done their own creative versions of the lift off, including this inspirational art by Carol Ann Rodriguez which ran in a national advertising campaign.

Andromeda Rex in a personalized, channeled painting by Birgitte
& Peter Fich Christiansen  https://fichart.wixsite.com/

## ESTABLISHING CONTACT – WHAT THEY DEMAND OF YOU

One thing almost everyone wants to know – how do I go about communicating with the Ashtar Command?

Admittedly some want to talk to the "big moon potato" himself, while others would be happy with a proxy underling. One of the tens of thousands of representatives under Ashtar's direct charge. All the sucking up or kissing lunar ass won't help if they think you are not worthy, or have nothing to offer them. They can be selective as ole shit if they are in that kind of mood, or they might welcome the opportunity to spend a little time with a dedicated follower. Sign up for one of the internet Ashtar sites and see what others are saying.

But here goes – let's give this very important topic a stab.

Before space aliens will communicate with you they must be certain of your motive and desire. They are not anxious for anyone to go out and make a "quick buck" off what they have to say. Nor do they wish to contact anyone who has only a frivolous interest in such matters. They are looking for people who understand their mission and can "get the word out." Though they will assist worthy individuals in times of great need, hey have repeatedly stated that their message is not just meant for a handful of men and women, but should be spread as far and wide as possible. Thus, when they do speak they will not usually talk on a personal level. What they want to get across is a lot more worldly in nature. Sometimes, they will help with personal matters if it involves spiritual development or a crisis that meets their requirements (centering normally around karmic influences). You shouldn't think of them in terms of having a few friends over to the house for tea. The Space Brothers have much to do and those who are assigned to help out on this planet must spread themselves "pretty thin" as it is. Thus, they take considerable care when it comes to speaking their mind. In order to "get through" to them you have to pass the test.

Through the spiritual messenger of Tuella (earth name Thelma Terrell, currently residing at the City of the Sun, a New Age community in New Mexico), we have been rewarded with a special dissertation on contacting the guardians who are trying to guide our development. This particular discourse was channeled through Tuella and comes from Andromeda Rex, Commander of a fleet of space ships circling the earth. His message will "clear the way" so to speak, so that you now will be able to approach the matter of attempting a space contact on your own.

## A DISSERTATION ON CONTACTING THE GUARDIANS BY COMMANDER ANDROMEDA REX

"There are five basic requirements which lead to successful communication between our dimensions, in conscious contact and telepathic thought exchange.

"First I would list QUALIFICATION OF MOTIVE. What is the motive in the desire? This should be carefully scrutinized and carefully searched by the participating soul. The desire must stand clean and undefiled by any self-centered purpose. The motive must be totally free of any desire for self aggrandizement or the flaunting of the self above others. The desire must be without any taint of launching a program that would return gain or fame to the souls so seeking. Wrong motivation will stop any seeker "in their tracks" toward advancement if it is born from an impure desire not in keeping with Light advancement upon the planet. Likewise, intellectual curiosity will bring no results whatever. Seeking in order to remove disbelief is another hindrance to results. One must believe in our presence before one seeks to converse with us. So let the heart be searched for perfect motive.

"Then, let DEDICATION BE THE INSPIRATION WHICH DIRECTS THE HEART IN OUR DIRECTION. The life and soul purpose of that one who desires our words must be one which has been dedicated to fellow men and the uplifting of the planet earth into its fourth dimensional expression and the fulfillment of the Aquarian Age on earth. For this we ever watch and monitor your world, seeking those hearts that are awakening to the greater picture, and the greater burden for a planet and its people. Those whose hearts bleed for the spiritual needs of humanity, and are dedicated to the coming of the Kingdom of God on earth, register our attention automatically.

"I am listing CONSECRATION as another basic requirement. This is an act of Love and Surrender of the human spirit to a Divine Purpose. Love is the strongest element in the Universe and the highest possible vibration upon your planet. It shines upon our monitoring board like diamonds across a dark sky. One who has begun to vibrate a life of Love to all Men, of all worlds, and is expressing that love to us in particular will in no way be ignored. That spoken Love will bring a like-minded response from our hearts to that one who seeks. For consecration added to dedication, builds a road or a frequency, along which our communications can travel back to the source of thought which has been projected to us. Thus as you lift your loving thoughts higher to us and our octave, you enable us to return our own along that same energy path back unto you.

**Hundreds may be channeling worldwide. The Ashtar Command can communicate over vast distances.**
**www.starmagichealing.com**

"Further, let me speak of CONCENTRATION. It is the nature of the human mind that it must be thinking of something, for it cannot be blank or motionless nor void. We therefore encourage concentration upon one certain thing, in order that mental activity in other directions can be erased. While one is thus concentrating upon one chosen thing, all else is shut out enabling one to subdue the busy conscious mind into stillness. Thus, if one will concentrate upon our ships in the higher atmospheres, thinking of our Love, our activities, and beaming Love to us in a quiet peaceful way, this action will be monitored and response will finally reach one who practices this discipline faithfully and regularly.

"I will close my thoughts on the matter by calling attention to MEDITATION. Now comes that moment of still waiting, that quietness within, like unto the quiet waters of a beautiful lake. Into this stillness, rigorously held intact by the mind, while in total physical and mental relaxation, will come the still small voice of heavenly response.

"Following these exercises one always gives thanks for that quiet moment spent with inner divinity, whatever its results may or may not have been."

**Science will tell you it's impossible for alien life to visit here from Andromeda because it is so far away. Did anyone bother to ask Andromeda Rex?**

One who has begun to vibrate a life of Love to all Men, of all worlds, and is expressing that love to us in particular will in no way be ignored.

**What can you do to "help out" the Space Brothers and the Ashtar Command?**

## "TALKING THEM UP"

### By Timothy Green Beckley

One of the reasons it is said that the government keeps a tight lid on UFO matters is because they are afraid of mass panic. Most often referred to is the 1938 "War of the World's" radio broadcast in which the moderator, Orson Wells, told of a fictitious invasion of earth by Martians. Many of those who turned into the Mercury Theater late and did not hear the beginning of the program thought that warriors from the "red planet" actually were attacking — and killing — innocent people.

The Space People do not want anyone to panic! The truth is they only wish to communicate with those who have opened themselves up and are willing to serve as channels. They are not anxious to barge into anyone's home uninvited. They wish to arrive as welcomed friends. In the messages beamed down to earth by Ashtar, commander-in-chief of the Free Federation of Planets, we are told that in order to be receptive we should think of them in a positive light and be willing to communicate on a first name basis.

"It is important to think of us in positive terms. We will come to those who do. (If you wish contact) think of us as if you know for sure we are real". To spark a contact Ashtar recommends imagining "a giant ship surrounded by a blue glow." He also suggests that people "make drawings of us and our craft. Tell people to look at UFO pictures." Ashtar also strongly advises that those attempting to communicate not be afraid to call them by name. "Tell them to think of Ashtar. Tell them to think of Aura Raines. (These are the names of various space people that have been encountered). Tell them to concentrate deeply on us. We will answer many of those who call. Tell them to have their tape recorders turned on so that they may record our messages. Tell them to get the word out."

Their ships come in many shapes and sizes, from the popular cigar to the bell shape complete with landing gear.

## PHYSICAL FORM

Though a great deal of their messages comes via mental telepathy to UFO contactees who are channeled into the proper wave lengths, from time to time as situations allow, they do appear in physical form upon our planet. This, I think, is very well demonstrated in the cases I provide in the chapter titled "*They Roam The Earth*." The experience of Oscar Magocsi in another chapter, "Inside the Saucers" pretty well illustrates what the space people are referring to when they say we should talk about them and "play them up". We shouldn't be shy when it comes to acknowledging their existence. In a sense it's time that all us UFO believers came "out of the closet" and let others know exactly what's going on. Oscar Magocsi had never believed in the existence of UFOs much less space people. That is until he had an encounter of his own just outside of Huntsville, Ontario, Canada. However, after this experience changed his life he began to seek out information, read books, attend lectures and ask questions. This open-minded attitude of a seeker of knowledge eventually lead to a face-to-face meeting with a space person by the name of "Quinten" and another alien named "Argus". If Oscar hadn't opened up his telepathic centers and indicated he was anxious to know as much as possible about UFOs and their occupants, he would still be peering up into the heavens looking for "lights in the sky," instead of talking on a personal level with our interplanetary friends.

George Adamski confidante Laura Mundo suggests "talking them up."
Perhaps they will be listening?

Laura Mundo, from Dearborn Heights, Michigan, has been involved in UFO related work for many years. Back in the 1950's she established the Flying Saucer Information Center and sponsored a number of public events. She once organized a lecture for the late George Adamski (a world famous contactee who claimed to have met a long-haired Venusian named "Orthon"), and over 5,000 persons attended. A charming woman (though upon occasion she has been known to over react emotionally), Laura says she knows what it's like to meet a real space person and has developed her own method for "getting in good" with them.

Her method coincides with what the space people have themselves said in many different communications — talk about them freely.

"Talk up to everyone that the space people are coming to remove those people whom they can in their insulated spaceships, as our atmosphere gets more and more unbearable because of the accelerating sunspot activity. Then one day it may suddenly dawn on you that you are talking to a real space person as they begin to ask very profound questions about outer space that only someone who has been there would know. You will know by that time that you are not to ask them who they are or someone might turn on them, but with greater training now from them, you should continue on with your job, talking-up the space people's coming and the emergency to the planet, perhaps lecturing, writing or in some other way getting their message across."

If you "talk up" the subject long enough, Laura insists they will eventually get the message and they will come to you "behind the scenes, face-to-face, as they have to me. And then the two of you will go on, perhaps together now...to 'talk it up.' There is time for nothing else." Like Adamski, Ms. Mundo professes to have conversed and met in the flesh "Orthon," a slender male Venusian with shoulder-length golden hair, and frail, but masculine features.

In 1958, Laura once again held a saucer convention and invited Adamski to speak as he had done years before. "Orthon, the man from Venus was there," Laura swears. "I was the only one to recognize him by his vibrations. He was a blue-eyed young man about five feet, ten inches, with a duck's tail haircut. He had beautiful white skin, although space people of all races are here. He nodded at me several times and smiled."

Almost two decades later, the same man looking exactly as he had in 1958, came to an event Laura was involved in. Laura was not feeling particularly well this day. It felt to her as if she were under "psychic attack, being drained of all energy. (As another person spoke into the microphone), I felt myself grow very sad, and sobs began to rise in my throat that I could not keep down." Laura maintains that she got the impression that something negative was trying to "possess me."

Laura left the stage actually screaming out in agonizing pain. "Suddenly this young man rushed directly from the audience to me. He held me in his embrace, repelling the negative power at once. He and my coworker led me to our booth and the curtained area behind it and put me on a couch. He worked on my neck until the pain entirely subsided. 'I don't know who you are, nor where you are from,' I told him, when I could once more speak, 'but I am very grateful to you.'"

Laura says the young man knelt down beside her, hugged her and proceeded to kiss her on the forehead. "He said 'God bless you,' and then left as quickly as he had come."

Laura's final words of advice: "Remember 'TALK IT UP,' LIKE WE HAVE DONE, IF YOU WANT TO BE 'TAKEN UP!'"

Keep the space people close to your heart and they will remember you. Think about them as you would your very best friends, because after all THEY ARE!

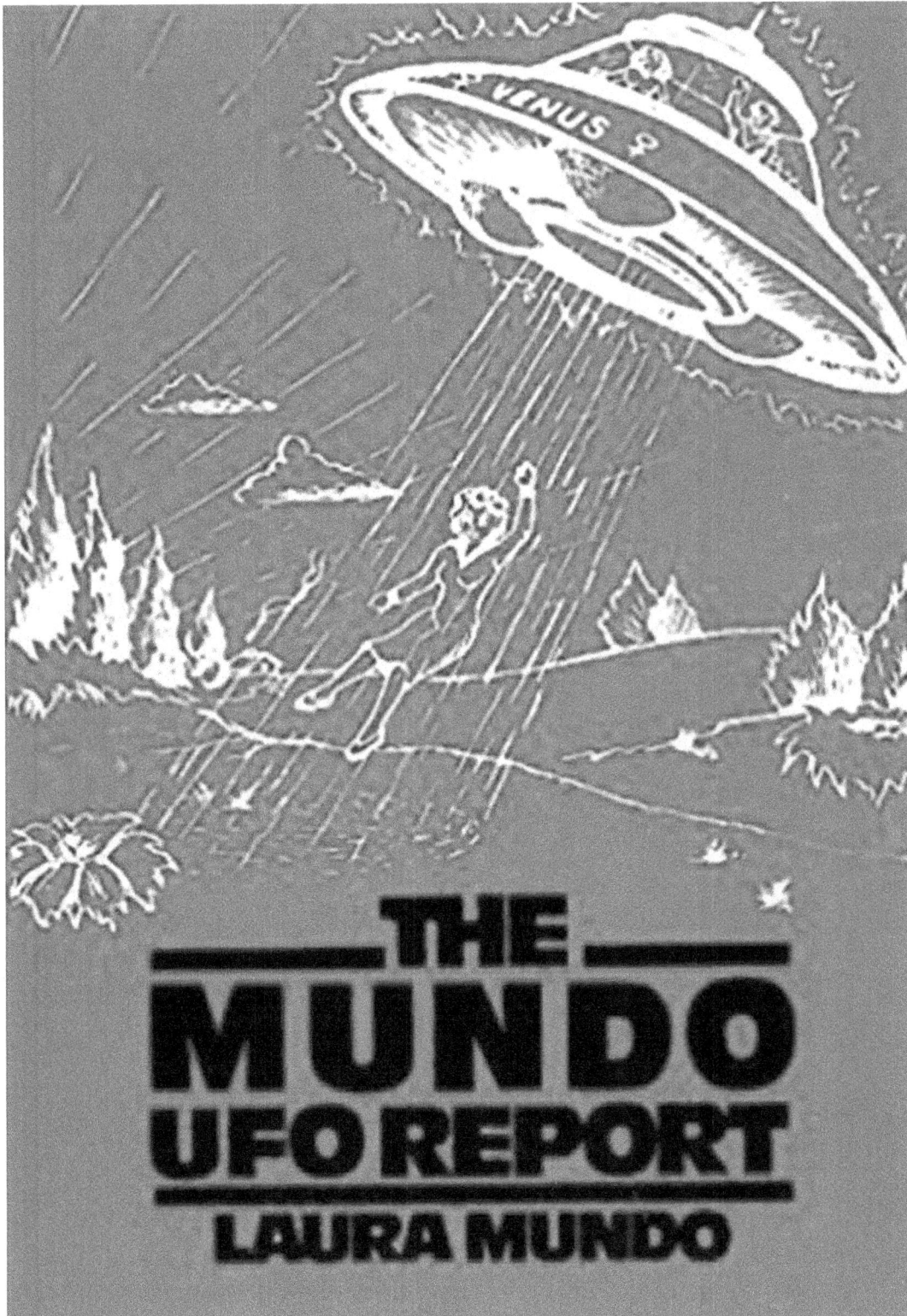

Laura Mundo was ahead of her time when she self-published "The Mundo Report."

The Earth will return itself to its true and pure natural state.
It will be a place of harmony and love, of lush green forests
and clean waters.

# EARTH IN UPHEAVAL, CLIMATE CHANGE AND THE IMPORTANCE OF DISCERNMENT
## By the Ashtar Command

I will speak about the options or choices that each of you will have, with particular focus on what we "have to offer." I have given considerable information on what to expect from the dark forces and from your government. Of course there is much more I could say on this subject. I do not wish to dwell on the negative aspects of the choices anymore than I consider necessary for your general information. To do so gives the potential of drawing those energies closer to you. This does not mean I wish to avoid mention of them. To speak more of the dark side's involvement at this time would not be a good service to you. I always suggest you protect yourself from any form of negativity, particularly those powerful energies we have previously mentioned. I have to maintain a certain balance with regards the information I may provide. I want you to know all that you wish to, yet much caution is in order when relating to the negative forces. I will continue to mention those from the dark side when it is appropriate. However, there is another side, that is the Light, us and countless other beings of light, who are willing to help when called upon.

As you should be aware the origination of humankind upon this planet came from the Pleiades. They have their own "history" from which they may draw many parallels to your present day Earth. Some people have suggested that they are from your future and say they have regressed to change or affect the outcome of certain events. This is only partially true. Indeed we are from your future in a certain sense. But all is now. We are all simultaneous. Therefore there is no real past or future, only now. But in a sense we are your future. I do not intend to make this complicated, as Tom has repeatedly requested that I keep it simple and in this I concur. But some things, no matter how simplified I see them, are very complex when viewed from your present perspective. So I often leave off certain aspects to keep it as understandable as possible. Others may in fact want the "uncut" version of what I say. This too I respect and often provide. However, if our truths are beyond your present comprehension, then it does little good to "impress" you with our expansive knowledge. I and your other space friends are of the Light and are the Light, the light of love. We have much love to offer you but we have learned through our own development that we can only offer it, not force it on you. There were times in our history, eons ago, that we too, were zealous with our belief systems. We evangelized and presented our heartfelt position to those who wanted them as well as those who did not. We were missionaries in our own right. We knew what was best for anyone, even those with a view different than ours. So this is just one of the parallels we can call from our own experiences.

We are now light beings or star beings if you prefer. We are pure love but not perfect love, as only the God Source can make this claim. But there are others who are "close" to perfect love. Here we speak of "perfect" as one of your limiting expressions. Actually you do not have a word that can properly describe our level of love. We are outside your comprehension. Yet we must relate to you as well as we can. From your limited understanding we are perfect love. The God Source is complete love which is perfect and total in every respect.

**The Earth must cleanse herself of the different levels of negativity. It will do this in a most natural way, by means of water, wind and fire. Indeed all the elements.**

As loving star beings, we offer our services to humankind and the Earth. We do this for no other reason than because we love you. And because we love you, we do not and cannot interfere with your spiritual growth and development. We have much to give you if you ask us, but it is a gift and does not have to be accepted. There is no good served, EVER, when the will of one is forced in any way upon another. Even if you see a person drowning and that person clearly defies any assistance, then to force your life saving techniques on this person does not serve any useful purpose. Many will object to this, but what I say is true. Of course in my example, you must completely understand that the drowning victim wishes no assistance. Each person's destiny is in their own hands. It is each person's responsibility to present only their own self, their own direction. Some gladly turn this over to others, for seldom do they understand the consequences of their own decisions.

We do not and cannot accept the responsibility for any energy except our own. This is why we do not infringe on or force our beliefs on anyone. Many in time may be taken in by the Reptilians, as they will not only appear to be helping humankind in general ways, but they will also insist on acceptance of their ways. If nothing else serves as a warning to cause each to think, it should be the insistence or forcing of beliefs on the people, by these or ANY energy. Most in this country and others are firmly convinced that it is necessary to help those who cannot help themselves, including those who do not even want the help. This attitude will fit well with the "help" to be offered by the Reptilians. On the other hand, this is not our way. It is not appropriate to interfere with your right to choose.

It is your free will to experience whatever it is you set out to do, as long as it does not harm another. It is your free will to not expect another to impose any belief upon you.

Humankind will be given a choice. The Earth has made her choice to move into a higher realm. But it cannot easily do this with the harm created by humankind. This includes physical and vibrational harm. Therefore the Earth must cleanse herself of the different levels of negativity. It will do this in a most natural way, by means of water, wind and indeed all the elements.

Much of this is not necessary as humanity alone can change into a more loving vibration. There are many physical Earth changes that must occur, regardless of what humankind does. These are for the purpose of realigning the Earth's balance for its new orbit around the Sun. But there will also come a time when humankind must temporally leave the Earth so the final cleansing can take place.

The Earth will return itself to its true and pure natural state. It will be a place of harmony and love, of lush green forests and clean waters. It is during this period of transformation that humankind must leave, for humans will not be able to withstand the cleansing powers as well as the 5th dimensional vibrational changes.

There will be choices to make, this is for certain. We have already given some perspective of what will occur if the dark forces are your choices. We are the positive, loving choice for those who can discern us to be so. It will not be necessary for you to believe in our ways, or to change your beliefs in order to make us your choice. You merely need to acknowledge that we are your choice and sincerely defy what the dark side may have for you. There will be opportunities for each to continue developing at whatever belief level you may have. This will be done elsewhere, but it will be allowed to be so. At the same time, those wishing to remove their limitations can do so. This too can be done without our assistance. It will be done without our interference.

It is not necessary that each citizen knows all the facts about what is to occur within your government. It is not necessary that each person knows all the details about the coming of the Reptilians. It is not necessary for these things to be known in order for each person to choose a path of love and project that as a part of mass consciousness. This would be most effective.

At the same time it is obvious to us, your space friends, that there has been considerable programming of each of you in those areas that do not normally cause you to wonder about beings from space coming forth, or lack of trust in certain elements of your government. So this creates a slight dilemma for us. We are not ones to go around "preaching" to get our message across. At the same time, we are well aware of the many potential Earth changes and the relative short time period for great change to and upon the Earth. So we have been asked by your Mother Earth for some assistance. We have been asked by your Sun to help those who would seek our help, if they but knew of our existence. And we have been asked by the God Source, the Creator of all things, to help in the most loving of ways to make the Earth's transformation into the 5th dimensional being a most pleasant and swift one, and at the same time to offer the same loving assistance to each on the Earth who will accept us.

We are of the Light and therefore we are love. In whatever way we offer our assistance to you, it must be known by all, that we give it to you without any requirements or conditions attached. We and our help need not be accepted. But this does not mean we will not be seen or even heard, outside of channelings such as this. There will be a time in the relatively near future that we will appear to the masses, just as we may on an individual level at this time. We tell you this so you do not believe we leave everything to your future imagination, as those from the dark side come forth when their time is right.

We do not intend to come as sales people, selling our services. This we want you to know. We are here in love now, and this will be so when our physical manifestations are to be. We wish to influence only your own self awareness, your own self love. Master Jesus taught these same loving principles to those on the Earth. Some listened, most did not. There has been a focus on the man called Jesus and not on what he really had to say. He spoke of love, but look around you and search for love. Most on the Earth know of Jesus, the man, but most do not know of love, his message.

We do not want you to focus on us as star beings, but as messengers and helpers. We want you to focus on the love, the Christ love, and not so much the Christ, and certainly not the different star beings who could visit you. This is one reason there are already many, many star beings among you. They are here to work WITH YOU and to help whoever will accept their help. They have come at great risk to themselves, for they are subject to the same physical laws, the same bombardment of non-love, and the same programming as all on the Earth are. These we tell you are your "walk-ins." These are those who are you and are us - we are all one. Many are now awakening to their origin. Many more will do so in the future. I must say that some will not choose the path they agreed to because of the strong influences of those things I have already mentioned. This possibility was recognized before the physical reality of their incarnation. Each is responsible for themselves, regardless. The dark forces are particularly adept at identifying those star vibrations and focusing their energies in various ways on these individuals so they may keep them from their agreed to path.

I tell you of these things so you will know the physical influences are potentially very great on those who have accepted the human form as their way to help. These men and women and children are not "supermen," but merely like each of you. They are here to help, just as we are, just as others in the human body are. It is not wise that I give the names, as some people may look up to them when this is not the intent, or others may target them for negative actions. You may ask and those who know will tell you. But it is not important who they are, but who EACH IS.

We do not present ourselves to most because most are not ready. We do not wish to infringe on or influence your free will to choose your own destiny. Over time many have closed off their spiritual awareness. In doing this you have lost your sense to recognize our non-physical presence among you. Many have lost that trust in themselves and their ability to discern the many energies that are now around you. For the Earth plane abounds with energies to help humankind, only most have accepted these as myths and not real.

These spirit energies are in ALL things, on and around the Earth. Most have grown to believe that "spirit" is an untruth. The word "spirit" is simply a meaning for the non-physical. You are now in the 4th dimension, but most view your surroundings and your thoughts from the 3rd dimensional beliefs.

As you can see, I can direct my words to so many facets of your human experience. This is easy for me to do when trying to inform you of what is happening around you. As I have said, knowledge of all things is not important in order to accept love, whether from us, the Christ, the Creator of us all or from all of our energies. But it is important for each to know discernment, that ability to recognize the energies of truth and love. It is not something you can get from these or any channelings. It is not available from your Bible or other holy books. It is not going to be automatic when you see our physical manifestations or the physical presence of the dark forces. Discernment is an ability each soul on the Earth has, but most have confused with judgment. It is your own, instinctive ability to feel or know a certain way. It is your own responsibility to develop, or not to do so.

I leave at this time. I do so in love for humankind, the Earth and for the One Creator of us all.

# Ashtar, Of The Ashtar Command

http://ashtar.galactic.to

There will come a time when humankind must temporally leave the
Earth so the final cleansing can take place.

Ashtar

Ashtar Intergalactic
Command

© Marc Brinkerhoff

Life like rendering of the Commander Ashtar by Marc Brinkerhoff based
upon face to face meeting.

# THE GALACTIC MISSION OF MARC BRINKERHOFF

## By Timothy Green Beckley

**I** have known Marc Brinkerhoff for several decades. Outside of the UFO connection, we are good friends. In fact, in a series of synchronicities (which have plagued my life and professional career), Marc met his life's partner through me. Phyllis was working as a producer at WPIX-TV here in New York. Phyllis was fascinated with UFOs. My "co-conspirator" and publicist at the time, Harold Salkin, was trying to promote me on the local media circuit when UFOs were still considered a novelty on the news and the many early morning chit chat shows. Phyllis was particularly interested in first hand experiencers which I was not, so Harold introduced Phyllis to Marc who had gained a reputation as a contactee who had the uncanny ability to aim his camera at the

Tim, Carol Ann and Marc at Pine Bush UFO Festival circa 2018. (Photo by Phyllis).

sky, snap the shutter of his "Nikon" and mysterious, "unknown" images would appear. In short he was an extraordinary photographer of what appeared to be spacecraft from other worlds and dimensions.

In short, Marc claims to be a Walk-In and conscious channel for the "Alsyglion Group" and has met Ashtar "head on," face to face. He is also a fantastic artist who makes the aliens, fairies and wild life he renders come alive on canvas.

## THE EARLY YEARS

Marc's first UFO experience took place on an athletic field near the Mahopac, New York high school. As best as he can recall, it was around 3 P.M. when he observed a large silvery sphere, "like the metal ball in a pinball machine. No sound was heard," but he does remember "receiving a feeling of great love from it."

Since that day, Marc contends, extraterrestrials have been contacting him and other humans. Apparently, they are programming us to save the world and the universe from possible destruction. He sees the aliens as being benevolent, human-like "Space Brothers" who are here NOT to harm us, but to lead us along the path to spiritual enlightenment and usher in the New Age. The mild-mannered UFO contactee further believes that in a previous incarnation he lived in another galaxy and that his mission in this life is to teach love to his fellow man. Marc says the beings he's in touch with come from the constellation surrounding the star Bootes. He further declares that he mentally talks to them and that they have appeared to him in the form of a white glowing light from which seven human-like forms emerged. He says they once surrounded him for 10 minutes to infuse him with love and then disappeared. Since then, Marc says he's been taking photos of spaceships some in remote places like open fields, and others right outside his apartment near Central Park in Manhattan.

Brinkerhoff spies on the sky, ready to take a picture at any given moment.

I am not going to dwell upon his unique, almost supernatural, talents here. Those wishing further details are invited to pursue them by obtaining a copy of our book, "*UFO Repeaters – The Camera Doesn't Lie!*" You will find it to be a hefty volume full of telling photographs by those like Marc who maintain a close relationship with the Ultra-terrestrials who it appears almost take their invisible "hands" and have them point their photographic equipment at certain sectors of the sky, only to have their craft pop up on film negatives, digital prints and video. It's bizarre. It's uncanny. It's got me stumped as I know that in most of these instances trickery and deception is not part of the formula.

## INTRODUCING ASHTAR

Initially, I hadn't considered Marc for inclusion in this book. I never really thought of him as an emissary for the Ashtar Command. And then one day he happened by "coincidence" to send me a portrait of Ashtar he had done and I said to myself, "This painting is so realistic that it's almost as if the artist was working with a live model." When I asked Brinkerhoff about how come this portrayal seemed so vibrant, so real, he blew my mind by telling me that "Oh it was nothing really," that he had met the Commander Ashtar on board one of their ships so he just drew it from memory.

Anxious to know more, even though the deadline for this book was coming up fast, we decided to quiz Marc Brinkerhoff on his involvement with the Ashtar Command. As it turns out, I am glad that we did since our conversation answers some of the many questions I know our readers must be asking themselves as they get hooked on the material presented.

**QUESTION:** You have graciously given us permission to use your pastel portrait of the space being known as Ashtar. Under what circumstances did you first come into his sphere of influence?

**BRINKERHOFF:** I feel like I have always known Ashtar. I see him primarily when I am on the teaching spaceships around the Earth, or on the 7th through to the 12th dimensional Intergalactic Spaceship at Galactic meetings in deep space. When Soul Traveling I appear in my higher self form (or as my 'true self'" in my 7 to 9 plus foot form near the Earth and our solar system's dimensions). I work with people who are spiritually aware and out-of-body when on the three teaching spaceships that are over different countries around the Earth. I guide people to areas of the spaceship where they may want to go to a class, or bring them to places where they can explore the ship more. The three inter-dimensional spaceships around the Earth are invisible from scientific study and telescopes on the dense physical levels.

Some of the information I will give to you is from my own personal physical encounter with Ashtar.

Some of the information I will give to you is from my own personal physical encounter with Ashtar and meetings I had during Soul Travel when connected to my Oversoul and working with Ashtar. Most of the information will be from my own Oversoul that I am connected to through what I call 'Conscious Channeling' or 'Conscious Viewing' as well as during Soul Travel. Basically, I can see through my own Omniversal ET 'eyes' on the 7th through 12th 'plus' dimensions when I consciously connect to my Oversoul. It is like being in two places at once. Some of the answers will be my experience and also deeper information from my Soul Travel experiences where I connected to my Oversoul, who has more information about Ashtar and who he is in this Galaxy and the Omniverse. When I am Soul Traveling all of this information is known to me in my 'Marc' consciousness that is aware and alert when on the spaceships. I am not always allowed to reveal or bring back all information to the Earth. My Oversoul will block some information from me at times, so I may not reveal anything prematurely

I drew Ashtar's picture based on a meeting I was attending in deep space with the crews from the 'Intergalactic Mission' in 2009, where he is leaning on his elbows seated at a large clear 'glass like' meeting table. I was sitting three people from him on his left side. Ashtar had finished speaking about some ideas he had regarding areas in other galaxies that are expanding and where people are having 'higher thought (that is one way the space people say...people are turning back to Creator and 'tuning up' more). Some of the people at the meeting had to leave and had already left the meeting room. (Now, at this time I was 'consciously lucid' that I was in the Galactic meeting as my "Marc" Earth self was connected and totally aware of where I was.) I was standing near the huge meeting table and was getting ready to leave the room soon, so I sent a telepathic thought to Ashtar saying, "That was an ultra mega download of info. Thank you, I will see you tomorrow." (On Earth we are used to saying tomorrow. The space people know what that means...even though they do not speak in tomorrows, but in spaceship processions if on a mothership, or a giant Arcvanna and it is similar to "days"...as in planetary rotations if we are near a planet.) Usually...'time' is set in our minds and all souls get a 'feeling' about 'time' in their minds and bodies.

It is the same way we speak about something happening a week from now (like a meeting, etc.), we all get the 'feeling', or 'inner sense' of the length of time it may take before it happens. As Ashtar looked up at me with that side glance he does at times...I knew he was getting ready to also leave soon. He telepathically said to me, "Yes, it was a tremendous amount to convey through thought and I have another meeting to get too soon on another ship in the galaxy. I will see you again next time you travel back to us from Earth." When Ashtar was looking up at me...that was the image that infused within my mind to show his endless compassion and love for all souls and people everywhere. I drew Ashtar from my memory and also from 'tuning in' to him. I see Ashtar occasionally teaching, training, or commanding some spaceships within the many Space Alliance Groups, or at Galactic and Intergalactic Meetings with the many galaxy groups that are within the 'Intergalactic Mission' throughout the Omniverse.

The Major Intergalactic Meetings are usually held three times a year (in Earth terms of a year), in deep space on huge Spaceships (from hundreds of feet in length, to many miles long), and on giant Arcvanna spaceships (that are bigger then planets), around the deep space areas of our galaxy and others. More Major meetings may be held if there are priorities that require new information, or urgent stellar or Solar Events throughout the galaxies, or within the Omniverse.

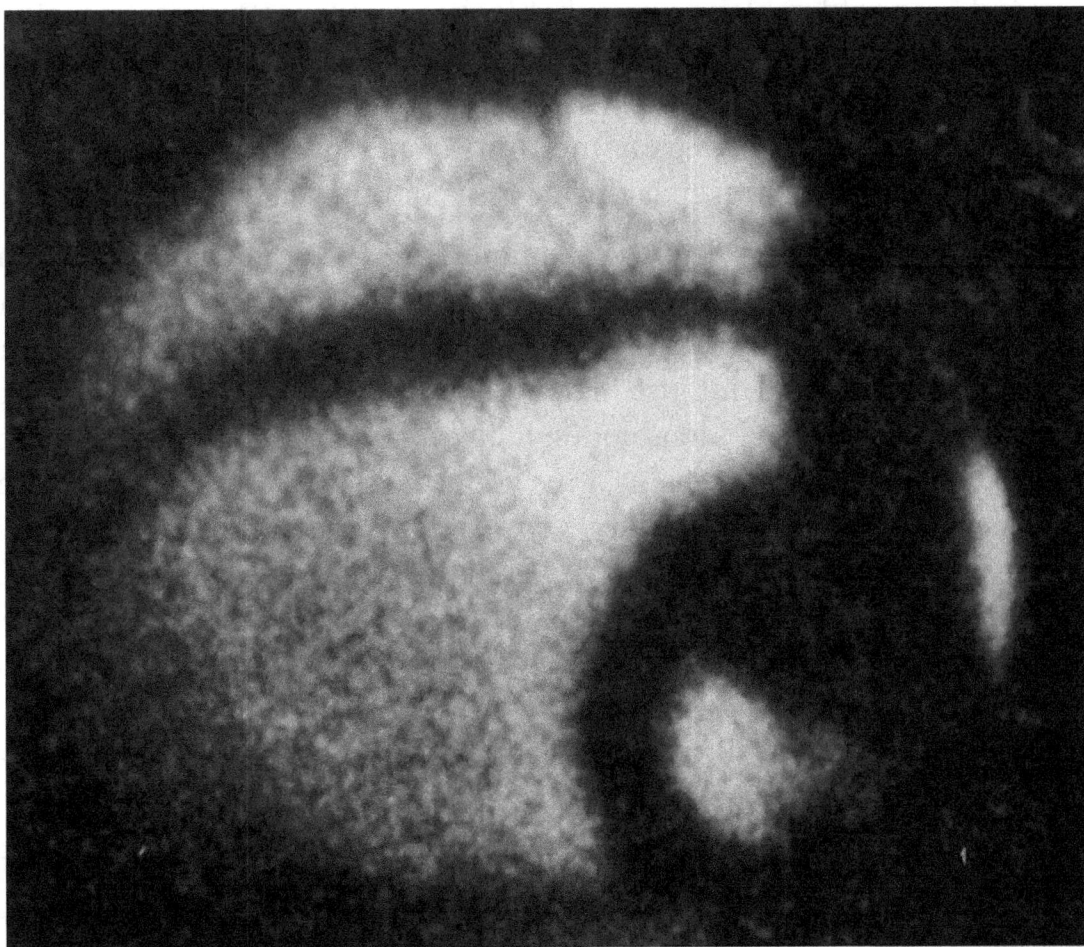

**Alien silhouette at a porthole window: Red scout spaceship and hatchways to a mother ship: This image was taken at the Mahopac Middle School field in Mahopac, New York, after 9:00 P.M. on Saturday, September 17, 1977.**

## WHAT HE LOOKS LIKE

**QUESTION:** You have met him in his physical form aboard the mothership? Can you describe his appearance.

**BRINKERHOFF:** Ashtar looks like the image I drew of him. His height can be from 7 to 12 feet in height (depending on what dimensional level he is working on at the time), when I met him he stood at least roughly 7 feet and 3 inches tall and he has a strong muscular body. When I hugged him my arms and hands just barely touched his shoulder blades. I understood telepathically that he had adjusted his high 'etheric body' to be close to seven feet on the slightly more dense etheric to physical dimension we were meeting in on the spaceship. I also felt that my body was adjusted to fit into the etheric level of the spaceship, so I could meet with him and some of my space friends (or crew friends who are over 8 feet tall or more), as well. Ashtar has high cheekbones, slightly elongated eyes, a medium tan, a strong jaw line and long golden blonde hair that looked similar to my pastel picture of him. His presence is trustful, commanding, confident and calming when I have met him during out-of-body visits to the teaching spaceships around the Earth, and on August 10, 2015 when I physically met him in person. Ashtar also has a sense of humor when I have seen him speaking at some of the galactic meetings.

Ashtar projects himself as an Adamic High Etherian Universal space being and he resembles a form he had on Venus many thousands of Earth years ago. He is known in space in the same way that his over soul appears, or looks on the Higher dimensions. He has kind intense beautiful blue eyes with flecks of turquoise in them. Ashtar usually has golden blonde hair to dark golden blonde smooth to wavy hair that falls from 4 to 8 inches past his shoulders. It is very rare when I have seen him in a shorter and layered hair style covering his ears and falling to his neck and top of his shoulders. Ashtar sometimes has a part on the left side of his head, but more often his hair appears to be brushed back (like in the pastel), with a windswept look. His skin tones have ranged from light to medium olive tones, to a bronze tan, and to a tan that looks like a tan reddish gold, or a light copper bronze. He is NOT what people call a 'Tall White', nor is he a 'Nordic' or 'Pleiadian.' Even though he resembles them in some ways.

Ashtar usually wears a blue spacesuit with a trim near the neck of the color, or a design that signifies he is in command of the ship. When he is visiting another spaceship, Ashtar will have a different gold pattern on the collar that shows he is a Commander in the Intergalactic Mission and with the many Omniversal Space Alliance Groups. The spacesuit in the picture I drew, is the type and color I usually have seen Ashtar wearing. There have been times at different meetings where he was wearing a golden shimmering spacesuit, silver white iridescent spacesuit, or a medium cobalt blue spacesuit.

## SOME SAY ASHTAR IS A MESSIAH

**QUESTION:** How about your psychic feelings toward him. Some say that he operates on the level of a Messiah.

**BRINKERHOFF:** My intuitive feelings towards Ashtar have always been family, protective and love like a big brother. When you meet Ashtar you sense his strong confident personality, love for all life, wisdom of the ages, and devoted love for our Infinite and Radiant Creator (YHWH, as the Triune Aspect Presence). In that respect, I can see how people may sense energy around Ashtar that feels like he is here to help and transform souls. In truth he is here in our solar system to help teach souls on the spaceships surrounding the Earth and to rescue souls from the dense physical planet incarnations as well. Ashtar has spaceships that can rescue people physically from planetary disasters, magnetic pole flips and more, but ONLY when the souls are energetically prepared for the frequency exchange that can teleport them to the spaceships. That is why people are 'tuning up' their auric energy and studying ways to raise their personal frequencies. Ashtar's crews can rescue innocent children who have not been corrupted by the negative and evil influences of the physical planet Earths population and many religious teaching systems. A soul usually must also be open minded to understanding life exists beyond the planet Earth and have a love for our Infinite Creator.

Ashtar also works closely with Sananda (known on Earth as Yahoshua), who is the Supreme Commander in charge of all Space Commands and Alliances throughout the Omniverse, and He is in full alignment with the Infinite Creator's Divine Will in Action. Sananda is the one and only True Messiah, who was known on Earth as Yahoshua (Jesus Christ), and He is known throughout the Omniverse as a direct 'Aspect' of Creator as the 'Son' who is personal to all souls.

Ashtar is closely aligned and works along with Sananda, who manifests an energy of love and devotion to Creator that will energize a vibrational frequency around a soul's auric field. That is the energy picked up by intuitive souls as to why Ashtar seems to give off a "Messiah like feeling" when they meet him, or tune in to him. Also, there is an overshadowing process of the 'Christ energy' that occurs when Sananda works with other souls.

## ARE ALL CHANNELERS AUTHENTIC?

**QUESTION:** Channelers around the world claim that they have acted as a vehicle to trumpet Ashtar's voice. They proclaim his existence to the world and issue forth with a variety of messages. How valid are these channels and can anyone learn to receive messages from space?

**BRINKERHOFF:** When I was soul traveling on the spaceship one time back in 2008, I asked Ashtar how many people he communicates to on the planet Earth. He told me there are right now seven people, (that does not include me, because I do not channel anyone), and he added that some people think they are channeling him, but he said...those may be playful entities trying to trick people. I almost never read channeled information, however some that I have read in the past from people who channel did sound like Ashtar speaking. There have been a few that I read years ago, that I knew were not Ashtar speaking at all. He usually does not speak in flowery terms like "my beloveds" or "my dear children."

Ashtar told me that when people have passed away on the planet Earth (like Tuella, who used to channel information from Ashtar many years ago), he will at times 'tune' into people that are trying to make a connection to him through their prayers and telepathic concentration.

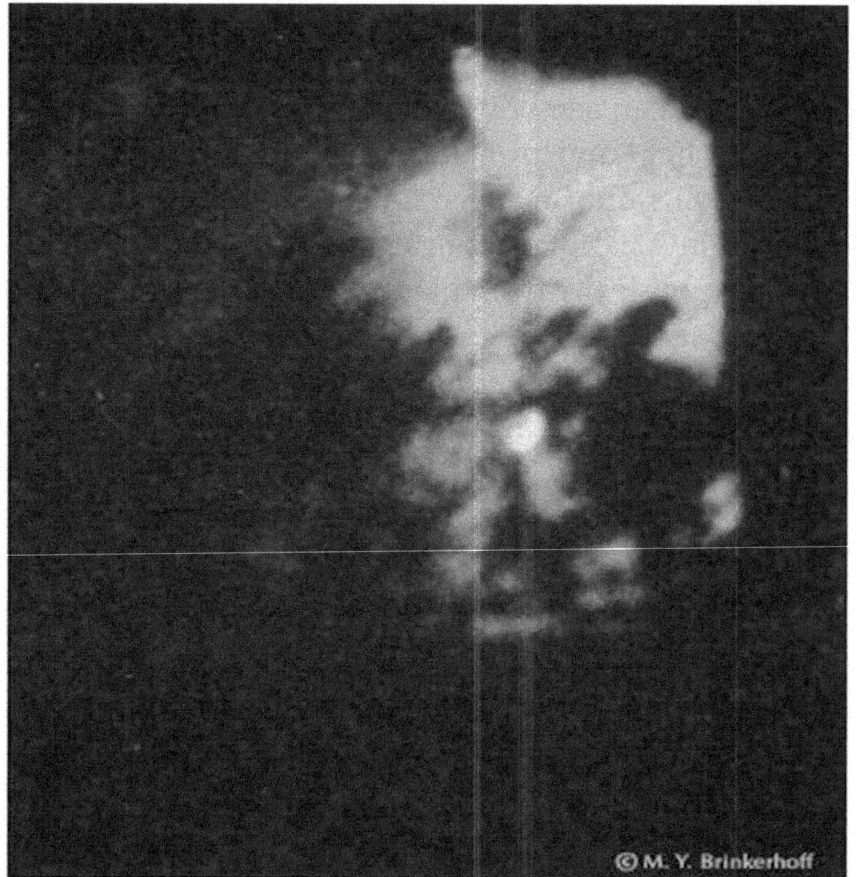

© M. Y. Brinkerhoff

Marc says, this photo "shows a spaceship window which is a square with slanted corners. (Or an eight-sided, square-shaped window.) Two space beings are silhouetted against an amber/orange background. The figure on the right appears to be sitting, while the tall, darker silhouetted figure on the left is standing. There is a ceiling-like structure and other background images as well. However, I also noticed the white spot in the center and was told that it represents the point of manifestation onto the film with their energy."

If he finds there is a past link to a soul (whether from past lifetimes on Earth, in space, or different planet systems in the many galaxies), he will meet with the person when they are out-of-body. Many times a person may never remember the experience with Ashtar, or they may just recall a glimpse of him in a semi lucid dream. Ashtar said he then will decide if a person is genuine in their truth, has little ego, is honest, spiritual and believes in Creator and life in space. He also looks to see if a person is truly trying to help others become more aware of who they are and their place and destiny in the universe.

I feel if a person is honest, truthful and not full of ego, but really wants to help people 'wake up' to the truth of who we are as souls and gain inner wisdom from Creator and open the doors to understanding the Omniverse, then people may tune in to their own intuition for spiritual directions. I personally do not like channeling because I know what entities can do to fake a session of channeling. People have to protect themselves first through prayer, Holy water and Holy oil to protect the soul from negative influences through entity possession, or negative attachment connections that can happen with unprotected channeling sessions.

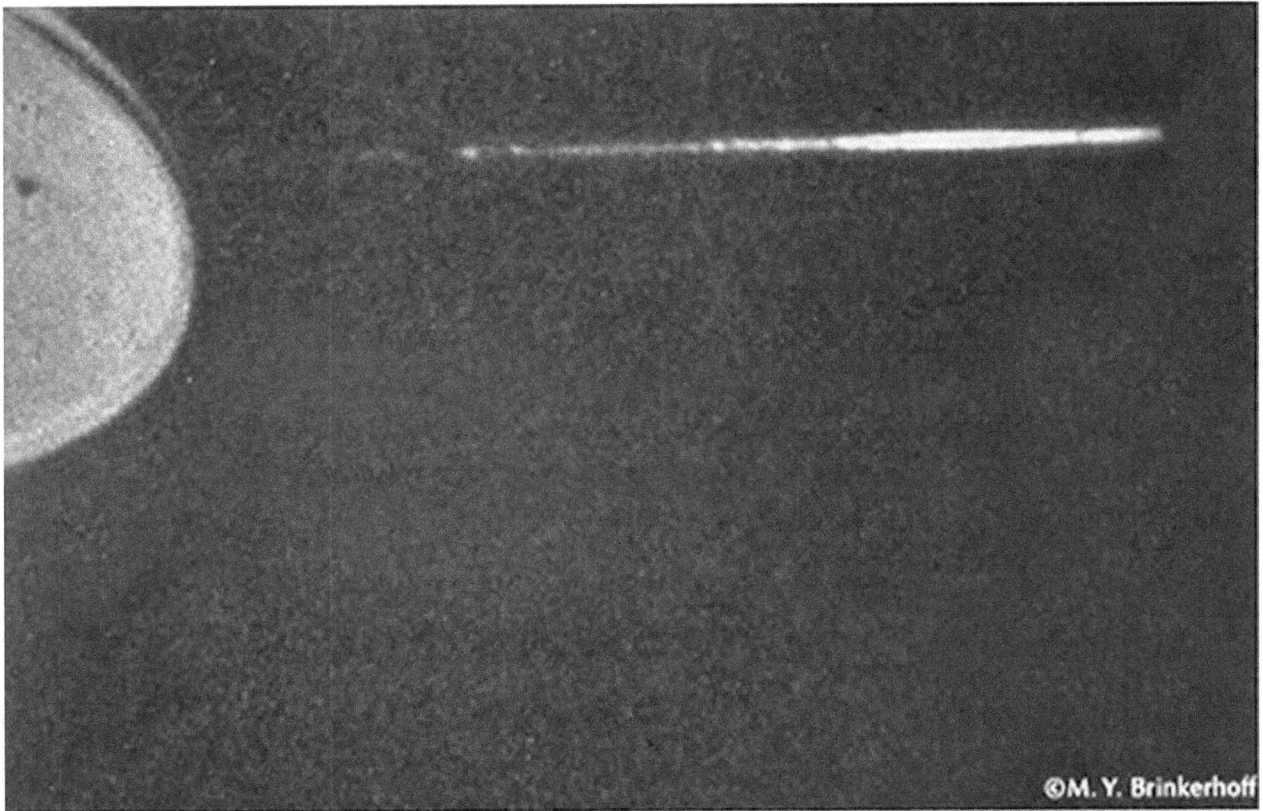

©M. Y. Brinkerhoff

This is an image of part of the under-flange of a spaceship (UFO) that is shooting a probe disc with a light beam trail.

## ASHTAR'S "SECRET" MISSION

**QUESTION:** What has Ashtar proclaimed as far as his mission goes? What topics does he seem most concerned about?

**BRINKERHOFF:** Ashtar is always fighting for good in the Omniverse. He speaks of his crews being vigilant about monitoring solar systems where war may start on dense physical planets. He has spoken about how atomic bombs and Nuclear bombs can harm etheric levels around the planets where other lifeforms are living. A nuclear war or small bombs being dropped on innocent people and property can damage other dimensions in the same area where a bomb exploded. Ashtar likes to talk about Solar Sun energy and the fluctuations of the star systems in the physical dense dimensions within the galaxies. The fluctuations can cause extinction events, or destroy civilizations. He travels a lot to different areas in deep space where stars are born and it is there where the plasma energy pulses to restore life on physical dense planet solar systems, as well as within other dimensions. He also researches the progression of the many thousands and thousands of galaxies that surround our own home galaxy.

## DOES HE HAVE A SPECIAL MESSAGE FOR US?

**QUESTION:** Do you have a short message that he has channeled through you?

**BRINKERHOFF:** Although I do not channel, Ashtar has told me information which is the same as the last question and helping people to understand the truth of who they are as a soul progressing through incarnations on Earth, and on planets in other solar systems throughout the millions of galaxies. Highly advanced benevolent extraterrestrials like Ashtar and his Intergalactic Command, along with other space beings from the Space Alliances...do not side with political parties on planets, or get involved in persuading souls to follow their ideas or beliefs. They will suggest a soul look at things in a universal view. It is also part of a "prime directive" for the space people not to interfere in a planet's affairs...unless they are specifically asked to give, or bring help by the main leaders of a planet, or a solar system.

Ashtar mentioned to me about trickster lower astrals pretending to be him and other extraterrestrials, angels, or religious saints when people were channeling. He said if an entity is making political comments, or telling people how to spend their money on stocks, or saying spaceships will hover over cities for a huge citizen 'contact', or more, through different people channeling...then people should be suspicious of whom they are really speaking with. I have heard there are different ways to "test the spirits'"before a person starts channeling. I feel people should research online and ask their trusted spiritual advisors questions regarding different ways of protecting a person from negative entities and demonic manipulation, which often masquerade as benevolent angels, extraterrestrials and spiritual beings.

The following process works for me when I am checking a spirits origin. A person can always 'test' an entity that comes through who says they are from 'space', or that they are 'Ashtar', or even a religious saint, etc., to reveal their true name and who they are in the Holy Name of Yahoshua Christ (Jesus Christ). The person must say it three times to the entity and demand an answer. If an entity does not answer...the person can cast out any entity that cannot, or will not answer. The person can also demand the spirit entity say the Name of Jesus Christ (Yahoshua Christ) out loud. Most evil entities cannot say the Name of Jesus in any way and they hate His Holy Blood, because they know Jesus (Yahoshua) is the Truth and they are to be cast out by the words from any soul who believes and knows the Power in His Name and in His Blood that was poured out for the salvation of all souls. If the entity says a name that is demonic, the person can cast the being away by saying, "In the Name of Jesus Christ (Yahoshua Christ), I now pour down upon me and all in my house the Sacred Holy Blood of Jesus Christ, and I bind you spirit entity as with chains and cast you into the outer darkness where you shall trouble not the seekers of Truth. In the Name of Jesus Christ be gone from me and all in my home! Amen."

Also, Ashtar always likes me to mention to people that when they are soul traveling (or astral traveling), they can see their 'past life' experiences on the three teaching spaceships Ashtar has stationed around the Earth. People can see their past life experiences through the Akashic energy frequencies that the spaceships 'computer like' systems can reach to show a soul who they are in the Omniverse. I have seen the areas in the spaceships where this is done in a chamber, or a very large room. The images can be seen like a 3D movie and watched from a seat, or experienced partially by the person watching while standing in the energy of the Akashic frequencies and feel as if they are reliving everything again, but they also can be watching from an observers perspective. The person can see where they chose well and where they may have made a bad decision in a past lifetime. It is really amazing.

## WHY DO THEY SEEM SO CONCERNED?

**QUESTION:** Why should the Ashtar Command be so concerned about our behavior when they come from such a far distance?

**BRINKERHOFF:** Ashtar and most space people consider all souls on the Earth and in space as family, or sisters and brothers. Ashtar has seen war and what happens to people after the effects of a war, or when other disasters have occurred on a planet. He has seen planets explode due to aggressive power and ego with a need for control, anger, rivalry, and jealousy. Ashtar and many of his space crews are here near the Earth and are working in our solar system and galaxy. They are not far away really at all. Our planet Earth is a dense physical training ground for souls and we are nearing the end of an age. Many prophesied corrections will be made in the not too distant future.

Ashtar and his Command are here to protect the Earth from negative ETs who want to control souls living on dense physical planets. Ashtar and his Intergalactic Command crews observe souls on the Earth that are awakening to spiritual understanding and are questioning their purpose in life, and have a desire to know the truth of who they are in the Universe. When people are out-of-body (or Astral Projecting), the benevolent space people on the spaceships near the Earth, will help guide and teach souls about their spiritual progression and more, if they have a basic interest and no fear of space or the universe. Ashtar and his space crews know the Earth is going through energetic frequency upgrades and that there are souls 'waking up' who need guidance.

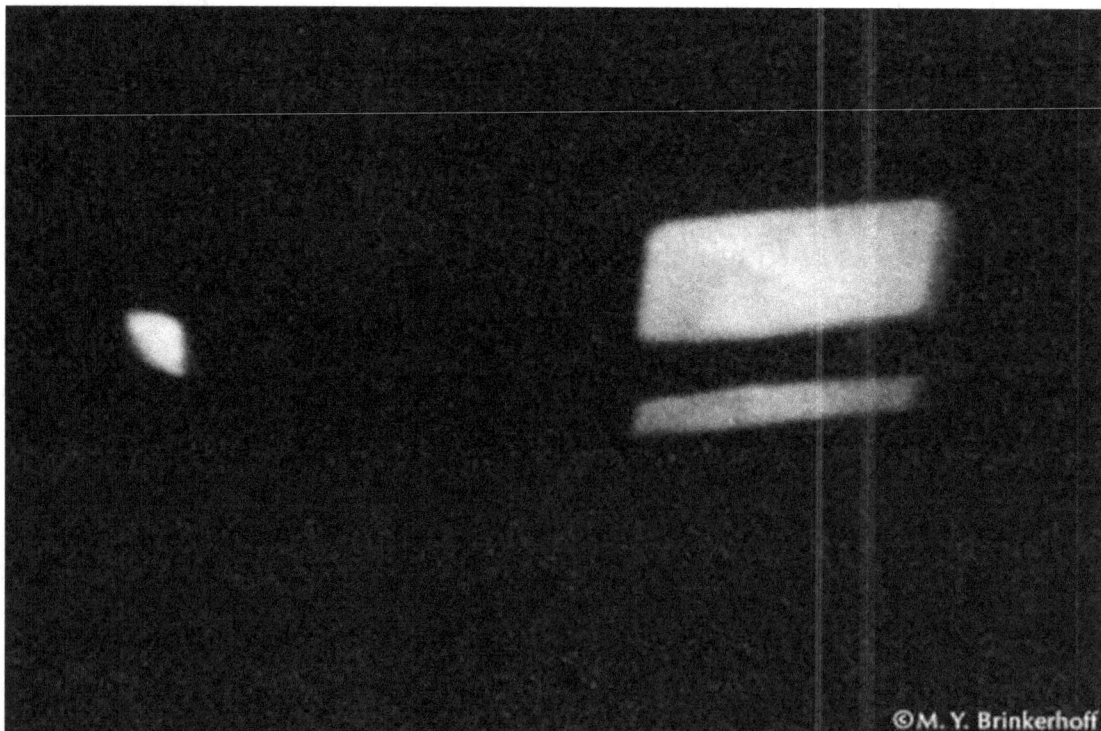

©M. Y. Brinkerhoff

Red scout spaceship and hatchways to a mother ship: This image was taken at the Mahopac Middle School field in Mahopac, New York, after 9:00 P.M. on Saturday, September 17, 1977.

The different benevolent Space Alliances and Ashtar's crews can dismantle with energy frequency beams any bombs, missiles, or more if needed, so that a planet will not be destroyed through a nuclear war, or other weapons of mass destruction that may cause an 'extinction event' chain reaction. Ashtar and the Space Alliances can intervene when the people on a planet may accidentally set off an energetic, or nuclear chain reaction event, where a planet may be destroyed. They can help because the energy reactions caused by nuclear, or atomic explosions can interfere with life on the different dimensions close to the physical Earth plane. The trouble is caused by the destruction of the cellular structures in the etheric realms and more, so there would be a massive re-balancing of the sonic frequencies again to recreate portions of areas in the dimensions affected.

## WILL THEY PREVENT A NUCLEAR WAR?

**QUESTION:** Can they halt our war-like activities, and lead us from negativity?

**BRINKERHOFF:** The Space people and Ashtar's crews are not allowed to interfere unless asked by the people on a planet (or leaders in a Solar System). Similar to the the old 'Star Trek' TV series where Starfleet had a 'Prime Directive' that the space crews were not allowed to contact a planet where the people were not advanced, or were still learning about life beyond their own planet. It is similar with our Solar System. ET space crews cannot interfere in planetary decisions where the leaders of a planet have war like tendencies. The benevolent space people will try to contact the leaders of a planet and offer to help bring healing remedies for all diseases and also to remove huge weapons of destruction, where a planet can be destroyed. If the people of a planet do not want help, then the benevolent space people will back off, continue to observe the planet and wait for a future opportunity to make contact again.

Many crew members from the Ashtar Intergalactic Command and other benevolent Space Alliance groups, attempt to reach their past 'family' and 'friends', who have become stuck in endless incarnations on 3D dense planets like Earth that exist throughout the galaxies. The ETs try to inspire them to seek higher spiritual learning through physical meetings when the time is right (like in a field, a store, or in a parking lot, etc.), or by working with them through lucid dreams and out-of-body experiences. The ETs have always told me that they will come to their own friends, meaning people they have known and worked with before. All people on the planet are not from the Earth alone, but have lived and traveled throughout space for millions of years. Everyone then is a soul and all have been extraterrestrials before they came to be born on the Earth at this time in the solar systems history.

Formation, Upper West Side, from living room window, NYC Nov. 1, 2010.

Golden Saturn UFO, Upper West Side, from living room window, NYC June 29, 2011 - movie film.

Morphing orbs with saucer shape UFO shot on Upper West Side, NYC, from living room window, Aug. 14, 2010.

Morphing saucer shapes shot from Cooper Union, NYC, on way to visit my friend, Ingo Swann on my birthday, May 18, 2012.

Saucer shaped UFO NY Botanical Gardens, NY June 8, 2012.

Morphing cylinder shape UFO Lexington & 86th bus stop, NYC, May 6, 2012.

MARC BRINKERHOFF
Conscious Channel, Contactee, Author
UFO Photorapher, Mystic Artist

7 morphing UFOs captured while in MOMA Sculpture Garden, NYC with 3 witnesses on Aug. 23, 2012. They moved too fast to catch much more.

3 UFOs traveling in formation captured outside my living room window on the Upper West Side of NY, Nov. 13, 2010.

This classic saucer shape UFO flipped over and tilted at me while I captured it outside my living room window on the Upper West Side, NYC July 16, 2012.

Morphing UFO, captured with 3 witnesses in Canaan, NY, July 27, 2011.

My wife shot this photo of me capturing the saucer UFO on July 16, 2012.

UFOs captured while visiting New York Botanical Garden, NY with 2 witnesses on April 19, 2012. They changed into a variety of shapes before disappearing.

MY PROCESS:
Often I am telepathically called to the window in my Upper West Side apartment to capture the ships. When I am walking outside, I am called to 'look up' in a particular direction and I will see them. Sometimes they come when I pray for them, but not always. I see way more than I am able to capture.

## THE AWAKENING OF HUMAN SOULS

**QUESTION:** Do they have an overall plan of operation?

**BRINKERHOFF:** I feel it has been answered already and that is to inspire souls who are 'waking up' to their true multidimensional Intergalactic Reality of their over soul or true self. All souls should love each other as they love themselves. We all should Love the Creator with all of our heart, mind and soul. Also, all souls should just follow the "Golden Rule," which is do unto others as you would like others to do unto you. Sananda, Ashtar, the Intergalactic Mission and many other Alliance space groups, have had the same plan operating for many, many thousands of years throughout the galaxies and in our Solar System as well.

## UNMASKING THEIR REPRESENTATIVES

**QUESTION:** The Ashtar Command is said to be made of representatives from many planets. Can you name a few of them? I have heard that Monka resides in the etherial on Mars and Athenia is Ashtar's soul mate. What numbers are here?

**BRINKERHOFF:** Regarding only the ETs from the Ashtar Intergalactic Command...currently there are very few physically on the planet Earth (maybe 10 to 20 people in a month or so), who come in physically to observe, or meet people through a personal encounter like I had with one of Ashtar's crew named Balthon in Central Park on August 10, 2015. After observing an area, going to a meeting, or when their mission is done (usually within 5 minutes to an hour in time), the ET will go someplace and dematerialize to go back to the spaceship, that is usually hidden from sight and hovering in the sky nearby. There also are many souls who have worked with Ashtar and work in their Higher Self forms on Ashtar's spaceships when they are out-of-body. I do know a few people who recall working on the ships through lucid dreams and out-of-body recall.

The ET crews working with Sananda and Ashtar throughout our Solar System from physical to dimensional levels range to well over 700 million, or more at different times.

Yes, I have seen Ashtar's Soul Mate and she sometimes has medium length brunette hair and other times she has long blonde wavy hair with green to blue green eyes. She usually has a medium golden tan to bronze skin tones. I recall Monka who also spoke to George Van Tassell, does live within our Solar System on a few bases and on a few planets as well.

All of the Planets in our Solar System have etheric and higher dimensional life on them, in them and surrounding them. There are cosmic to universal levels beyond the dense planet energies too. The dimensions go way over the 7th planes and on to the 12th and 22nd and more dimensional planes. (I used to speak of the dimensions over the 12th when I was in the 6th grade in the 1960's and also on radio and TV shows from the late 1970's and on to modern day programs and YouTube videos.)

There are many ETs in our solar system on many dimensions. Our own Moon has a base inside of it with physical and dimensional ET life as well working in and around it. I have visited the base when I was 5 years old and remember it. Our Earth has ancient bases inside the planet and dimensional ETs work on bases within the Earth. Venus has life inside the planet and in dimensions around the planet as well. Mercury has a base inside that is multi-dimensional and used to observe the Sun and solar activity. Mars has life inside areas of the planet and still has a base inside as well, and the two disguised moons have physical and dimensional bases inside them. Jupiter has life on many dimensional levels, or frequencies in and around the planet. Some of Jupiter's moons have life in bases inside and dimensional life in and around the moons. Saturn has dimensional life in and around the planet and inside some of its' moons like Titan. There are bases as well on a few other moons near Saturn. Uranus has etheric life on fine dimensional frequencies in and around the planet and there are physical and dimensional bases inside some of its' moons. Neptune is similar to Uranus and Saturn and it also has a few moons that have bases in them like Triton. Pluto has a base inside as well and dimensional life around it too. There are a few other larger planets beyond Pluto with dimensional bases in them and some ancient physical bases still being used inside of them.

The Sun is active on multiple dimensions and the Angelic beings move and love to be within the stars. ETs can visit stars on spaceships within many dimensional levels. There are bases in our Sun and other stars on high dimensional frequencies that have been set there by High Angelic beings in their thought projections. Souls can visit and feel the energy of a star through out-of-body projection and Soul Travel.

There is a planet named Talaron in the Andromeda Galaxy in a star system called Phenarrius, which has many people living on different dimensions and in physical form as well. There are many planets I have been on in our own galaxy and I have too many to name them here. I also want people to know that no matter which dimension a soul is in, or visiting through Soul Travel...we are physical in body form too.

## CLOSING REMARKS FROM TIM BECKLEY:

Marc, I want to take this opportunity for getting your position on these matters concerning Ashtar and his command across to us. I know our readers will absorb this information and apply it to their own lives. You take a very positive approach and may Ashtar continue his fine work if, indeed, he is overseeing the planet.

- All photographs in this chapter Copyright © by Marc Brinkerhoff.

## SUGGESTED READING AND LISTENING/VIEWING

**Websites: *marcbrinkerhoff*.com – intergalacticmission.com**

**Marc has his own Face Book page and lectures in NYC.**

**Audio and Video YouTube**: Do a general search for Marc Brinkerhoff or check out "Mr UFOs Secret Files" for our "Exploring The Bizarre" interviews with MB. KCORradio.com also archives the shows as does Stitcher, iTunes and Google Play.

### *UFO REPEATERS: THE CAMERA DOESN'T LIE*

Back issues of "*UFO Review*" and "*UFO Universe*" also contain his photos and dramatic stories. Possibly available on eBay.

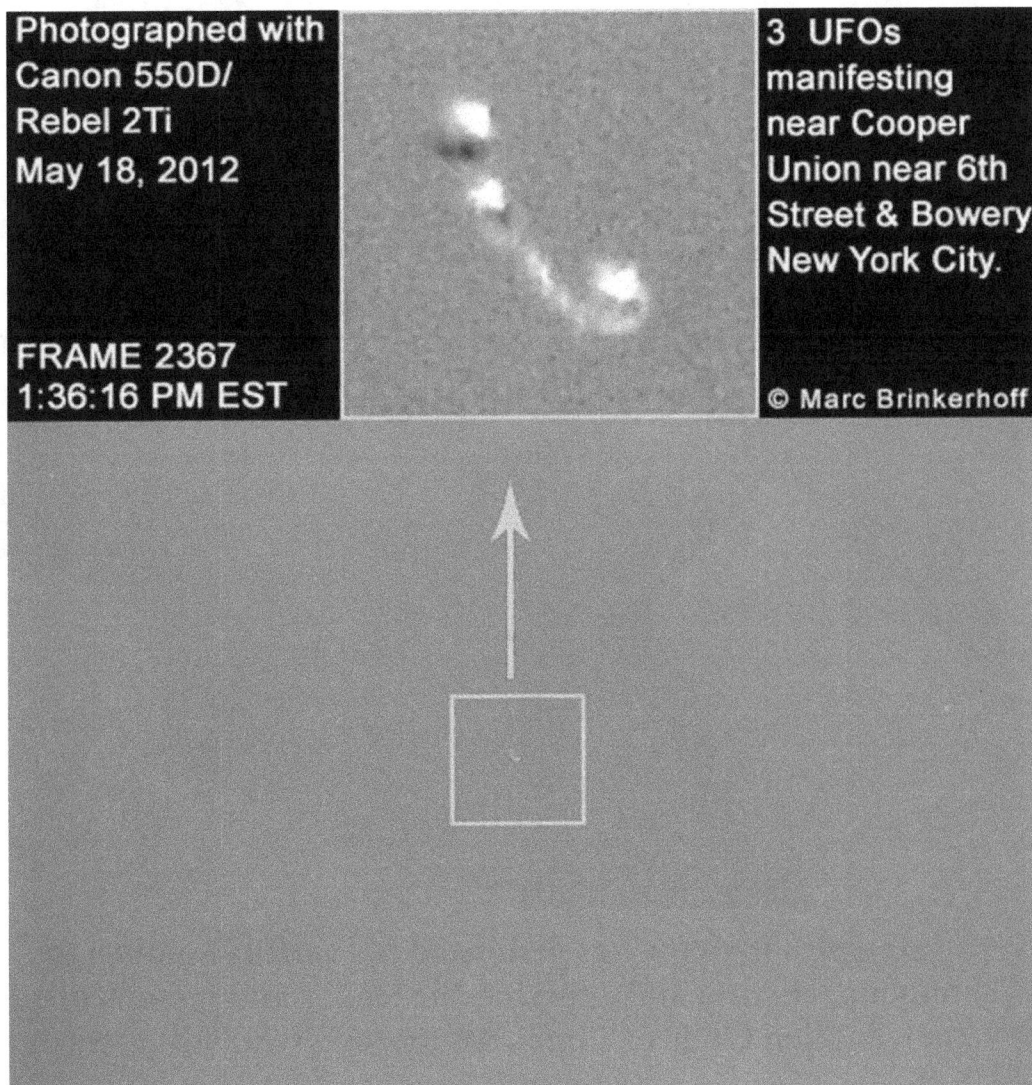

Photographed with Canon 550D/ Rebel 2Ti May 18, 2012

FRAME 2367 1:36:16 PM EST

3 UFOs manifesting near Cooper Union near 6th Street & Bowery, New York City.

© Marc Brinkerhoff

Over the years, Marc has managed to take some amazing UFO photos over New York City.

Hercules Invictus has dedicated his earthly sojourn to studying, sharing and applying the legacy and lessons of the ancient alien Gods of Greek Mythology who still reside on Mount Olympus.

## SPACE GODS STILL SPEAK
## An Olympian Exploration of a Curious Tome
### By Hercules Invictus

### APOTHEOSIS

*You will find a spring flowing to the left of Hades' Halls and beside it a white cypress tree. Do not approach these waters at all lest you be tempted to drink, for your thirst will be great.*

*You will soon find another spring, one fed by the waters of memory rather than forgetfulness. But before you can sample the cold waters rushing forth you must confront the Guardians.*

*They will block your way and point to the cypress tree. And you will be tempted to turn back and drink of those waters, for your thirst will be great.*

*Instead you must declare: I am a child of Earth and the starry Heavens, but my origin is Celestial alone, as you well know. I thirst only for my lost memories as I wish to awaken.*

*They will then allow you to pass and drink deep from the divine waters. Afterwards you will reside with the other heroes in Elysium. No longer a mortal, you will have become a God.*

Poetic Interpretation of **An Orphic Fragment** by Hercules Invictus

### BEINGS OF LIGHT

The light is white and blinding. I avert my gaze out of necessity, making it even harder to see the humanoid entity (or entities) I am communicating with. According to **Space Gods Speak** he is an Etherian from an unnamed world (one of three) in our Solar System.

***Space Gods Speak*** was channeled by the late Adelaide J. Brown of Los Angeles, a highly respected New Age luminary back in the 1970s and 1980s. Her transmissions from *The Solar Council,* the planetary leaders of our Solar System, were widely circulated to local UFO groups but difficult to obtain further afield, especially after the passage of time. Timothy Beckley collected and published the messages in 1992 with intuitive artwork by Carol Ann Rodriguez.

Carol's art was very helpful in establishing contact with the Etherian Beings of Light (henceforth BOL) as well as the other Celestial entities whose words are preserved in ***Space Gods Speak.***

In executing my initial contacts I relied heavily on the text and drawings, but eventually I could contact the beings directly, without the use of the source material. The beings seemed to welcome further interaction and proved very helpful in establishing and facilitating our continued communications.

The BOL before me seems to possess infinite patience and radiates an aura of all-encompassing benevolence. According to the original transmissions, people who live on his level no longer need to be housed in Tabernacles of Flesh and dwell in realms that can best be described as Heavenly. Nonetheless, they seem very interested in, and aware of, what we are, have been and will be doing here on Earth.

What follows is a sample of our exchange:

*Me: So I am to understand that routinely using affirmations that proclaim our divine origins and true nature are useful because they are sure to provoke negative reactions from within.*

**Being of Light (BOL)**: *Yes, that is correct.*

*Me: And why would I wish to deliberately provoke internal negative responses?*

**BOL**: *To bring them to light.*

*Me: I don't understand.*

**BOL**: *To see them clearly, to acknowledge them, understand how they came to be and then release them, freeing yourself from their unseen, and often insidious, influence.*

*Me: Understood!*

**BOL**: *May all we share be conveyed as effectively.*

And I actually did understand. When engaged in the intense internal work demanded by the practice of Olympian Shamanism, I have, on occasion, re-experienced childhood traumas through the eyes (and perspectives) of my adult self, allowing me to dismiss many festering inner hurts as not actually being as bad as my childhood memories made them out to be. These experiences tended to be profoundly transformative and liberating.

*Me: So this is, in essence, the equivalent of the Twelfth - and Final - Labor: facing one's deep-rooted darkness and emerging fears head-on and then bringing them up to the surface, like Cerberus, to and then through the metaphorical Lion Gate of my Heart.*

*BOL: Yes, this is indeed so as it relates to your own understanding of the Path of Apotheosis. And, in fact as well as in fable, as the result of this Labor's completion, Theseus is freed from the grips of Forgetfulness and reclaims his throne in Athens. The Lion of Olympus completes his imposed Labors and remembers his place on Olympus.*

*Me: Thank you! I will reflect on your words and continue to practice this technique until it ceases to produce results.*

*BOL: You are very welcome! May all our interactions prove as productive.*

The BOL seems to look up then extends its arms as if bestowing an Olympian Blessing. It increases in brightness, becoming One with the light, then both slowly fade away.

In gratitude for the insights I received, I utter my Olympian Prayer and, as is my custom, direct the lingering energies to any who may have need of them:

## OLYMPIAN PRAYER

*I call upon Heaven and the benevolent Powers*
*that shaped us in the dawn of time and guide us still*
*to bless this planet, its people, and all that they hold dear.*

*May all be blessed with optimal wellness,*
*with abundance and prosperity,*
*with love and peace, with joy and fulfillment!*

*In the name of the Highest,*
*I dedicate myself toward this becoming so.*

*And from the altar high atop Mount Olympus,*
*my soul's true home,*
*I sound the Horn of Summoning*
*and welcome all who heed the Call.*

*May it indeed be so!*

In **Space Gods Speak** the communicating Etheraian drew parallels between Beings of Light and the disembodied dead between incarnations. In Greek Mythology, Zeus revealed himself to be a BOL when asked to appear in his true guise to Semele, mother of Dionysus (a demi-god who later achieved Apotheosis, earning his way into the Dodekatheon). And Hades, the Lord of the Underworld, was also known as the Cthonian Zeus.

Though there were still many unanswered questions, I had more than enough to work with... for now.

## A CURIOUS TOME

**Space Gods Speak** is a series of channeled transmissions from the planetary rulers of our solar system who, as a body, are collectively known as The Solar Council. I had first heard of these transmissions back in the 1980s but was unable to track down any copies. I was overjoyed when Tim Beckley collected and released them as a book in 1992 through *Inner Light Publications*.

Rumor had it (back then) that Tuella, the well-known Messenger of Ashtar Command, had served as the vehicle for these transmissions, and that they were exclusively distributed to Ashtar Command groups. Though I had a friend in Southern California and one in the Ashtar Command at the time, my quest to track them down came to naught. As previously noted, they were in truth channeled by the late Adelaide J. Brown.

Within the pages of **Space Gods Speak** we are treated to the words of our planetary deities. Pluto, Neptune, Uranus, Saturn, Jupiter, Mars, Venus and Mercury all address modern day humanity and share their timeless perspective. The Solar Council that they preside over is also called (elsewhere) the Olympian Council, the Planetary Council, the Council of Elohim, the Wandering Stars and the Astra Planeta. The Space Gods are also known as Archons, Olympick Spirits and Planetary Spirits.

In **Space Gods Speak** each of them admits to being the actual entity upon which the Greco-Roman myths are based and each seeks to correct some of the distortions in their legend. Some, like Aphrodite, are very much like you'd imagine - save that she's the goddess of the higher octaves of love rather than of physical lovemaking. The Ancients knew her as Aphrodite Ourania (the Heavenly Aphrodite). Others, like Pluto, are very different from their portrayal in the tales.

The Olympians invite us to awaken to our multidimensionality, reclaim our divine heritage and join them on their home planets where we will discover that they are indeed our kin and not much different from ourselves.

The planetary gods are one with their planets and all are also physical beings encased in flesh. They are Celestial Elders who care about the problems perpetually plaguing Earth and send the transmissions to announce their presence and offer a helping hand. Many of them have been through, and have evolved past, many of the negative conditions we consider inevitable and inescapable.

Folks who are familiar with the teachings of the Space Brothers, Ascended Masters, Angels of all ranks, Spirit Guides and the humanoid Aliens of early Contactee literature will find much that is familiar here.

The Olympians are very much aware of our comings and goings and express themselves through the Abrahamic terminology and symbolism that dominates our culture. They also echo Ascensionist (Theosophic) teachings on the nature and purpose of our spiritual journey and our eventual return to the exalted estates from which we fell.

Though these concepts seem to be purely New Age, some of them were actually expressed in Greco-Roman antiquity:

- The association between certain gods and the planets of our solar system originated in ancient Babylon. The Ancient Greeks adopted and adapted this system, which provided a way of identifying the gods behind their cultural guises and better understanding their spheres of influence and relationships with one another.

- Powerful entities were often considered one with the domain they ruled. An example is Hades, who is both the King of the Underworld and the Underworld itself. Another example was the River Styx, who was also a Titaness.

- The Planets, as Astra Planeta or Wandering Stars, were considered to be the bodies of the gods or their chariots. In the **Homeric Hymn to Ares** (Hymn number 8), for instance, Ares is praised for driving his luminous orb through the constellation-filled sky. It also links him to the space above the third Heavenly Arch (Mars).

- In antiquity mortals could communicated with the gods through their Oracles (channelers). Famous centers of Oracular activity that are still known to us today include Delphi (primarily Apollo and Dionysus, before that Gaia) and Dodona (primarily Zeus).

- Ancient Roman Science Fiction included trips to the Sun and Moon and interactions with Solar and Lunar inhabitants (as well as with denizens of the upper atmosphere). Lucian of Samosata's short works, **A True Story** and **Icaromenippus,** survive to this day. They read a bit like the **Hitchhiker's Guide to the Galaxy** books of Douglas Adams.

As stated, the material in **Space Gods Speak** is channeled, and like all such writing the message occasionally suffers from distortions and occasional repetitiveness. I myself was a channeler in the 1970s (and some have argued that I never stopped being one) so I know about the practice from personal experience.

**Space Gods Speak** is a unique and useful document. I salute Timothy Beckley and *Inner Light Publications* for preserving it and sharing it with a much wider audience (including myself).

## ASHTAR COMMAND

Despite not being authored by Tuella, Tim Beckley identified **Space Gods Speak** as *An Ashtar Command Book*. For the sake of thoroughness I wished to further explore the connection between the book and the UFO-driven initiative. My outreach to Ashtar Command groups was initiated a year or two after I had read **Space Gods Speak**. Alas, my friend had long since left the movement and Tuella had passed on.

Ashtar (aka Ashtar Sheran) was first channeled by George Van Tassel in 1952. He has since communicated with many individuals and groups worldwide. The Ashtar Command has been assigned to Gaia to assist in humanity's ascension into higher spiritual dimensions (apotheosis).

Years passed. I read some books and later scanned through numerous websites and online forums but, alas, I was never quite able to establish a viable relationship or resonance with any Ashtar Command group here on Earth.

In time I managed to gain an internal connection through the practice of Mark-Age spiritual techniques. I discovered that a solid foundation of cooperation and mutual support exists between the Olympian Council (aka Solar Council) and the Galactic Federation of Light. Several Ashtar Command vessels were assigned to us in 2015 after a new mandate for our mission was issued by the Elders on Neptune, which was later ratified by the Olympian Council.

Carol Ann Rodriguez's rendition of the God of Neptune in **Space Gods Speak** is very close to the Golden Giants I have encountered and communicated with in my Astral Journeys to that planet. This sketch also approximates the descriptions (and location) of the beings identified as Golden Giants in the Mark-Age revelations.

At present our relationship with Ashtar Sheran and the Ashtar Command remains on the Etherian (Aetheric) levels. I can sometimes sense them but we don't seem to interact much (unless our interactions are hidden from casual memory, which is sometimes the case). We are not an active part of, or currently coordinating efforts with, any terrestrial Ashtar Command group, nor does our Olympian Outreach effort distribute their literature.

## BEYOND SPACE GODS SPEAK

If you wish to continue exploring the mysteries of the Olympian Space Gods, I'd like to suggest starting with the following two books:

*Odyssey of the Gods* - By Erich Von Daniken.

Aside from Space Gods, Greek mythology is full of tales of sentient orbs and golden sky-chariots, wondrous robots and human hybrids, selective breeding spanning generations and voyages to Other Worlds beyond the veils which billow on the borders of our perception.

No wonder Erich Von Daniken, our planet's greatest proponent of the Ancient Astronaut theory, found strong support for his views in the pages of the Argonautica, the Iliad, the Odyssey, Critias and many other works of ancient Mediterranean authors.

Von Daniken cross-references his Hellenic findings with antique material from all over the world. Ancient people have left us an overwhelming amount of information about super-human beings with advanced technology who came from the heavens, lived on mountaintops, warred amongst themselves, taught civilized arts to our ancestors, interbred with mortals to produce kings and heroes, then vanished – after vowing to someday return.

There is a lot of interesting material on the Sacred Geometry of ancient Greek sites, the mysterious mechanical fragment from Anticythera, Stone Age cyclopean masonry, the remains of Giants, the riddle of Troy and Plato's Atlantis.

***Alien Space Gods of Ancient Greece and Rome*** - By W.R. Drake with Timothy Green Beckley and Sean Casteel

W.R. Drake's previously published books on Ancient Astronauts were an essential read when I first started exploring this topic in earnest. I had always hoped that he would spend more time on the Olympian accounts and was pleasantly surprised when he actually did. My delight was doubled when I discovered that that this long-desired work was published by the same folks who brought us **Space Gods Speak!**

Drake's work supports the assertion in **Space Gods Speak** that the gods of old are beings of flesh and blood and he weaves together colorful threads from many ancient accounts.

In *"Will the Gods of Old be Returning in Full Force Soon?"* Sean Casteel provides many additional insights and information that greatly expand the scope of Drake's work, extending the inquiry into the Greece and Rome of modern times.

An aside from the *Introduction*, which reveals the tale of how this tome came to be, Timothy Green Beckley shares his psychic adventures with a Greek sensitive at a sacred site in *"Revelations of the Oracle of Delphi."* Timothy is an historian in the mold of Herodotus and his companion is very much in tune with the civilization-guiding currents of Olympus.

## BUT WAIT, THERE'S MORE . . .

Pride of Olympus is our Merkaba, our Sun-Chariot, our Celestial Barge, the Wheels-Within-Wheels shamanic vehicle that facilitates our journeys to the Astral (Starry) Realms of Gaia's World Tree (our Solar System).

Pride of Olympus is our metaphorical vehicle for exploring various thematically related but seemingly different approaches concerned with explaining our human origins, guiding our human development and actualizing our maximal potential.

Pride of Olympus supports all of humanity's efforts to transcend this world and venture forth into the great beyond, be they metaphysical, mechanical or even imaginal.

Like all Astral Conveyances, the Pride of Olympus can - and does - assume many forms... including a weekly podcast!

Join us LIVE every Thursday from 9-11 PM EDT on the Spiritual Unity Radio Network to explore Cosmic Mysteries and hear the **Space Gods Speak**!

www.blogtalkradio.com/surn

Please Note: Pride of Olympus is also available On Demand through the same link!

Now go forth... and create a better world, one filled with Light and Love. On behalf of the Pride of Olympus and her crew, may your journeys be joyous!

Onwards!

# Hercules Invictus

Larger Than Life Living in the World Today - © Hercules Invictus

*Hercules Invictus is currently involved with several social causes, teaches, conducts workshops, hosts The Elysium Project, Pride of Olympus and Voice of Olympus podcasts. He occasionally writes for magazines, has published two e-books and has regularly contributed Olympian content to Timothy Beckley's paranormal anthologies.*

*Hercules most recently established the Order of the Golden Fleece and has been recruiting Argonauts to help him usher in a new Age of Heroes.*

*For more information please Friend him on Facebook, visit his website: www.herculesinvictus.net or e-mail him at hercules.invictus@gmail.com*

ASHTAR—COMMANDER IN CHIEF

## A TOUR OF THE PLANETS

**S**ome years back, a series of booklets were published that made the rounds of UFO and New Age communities. These booklets contained information that had been channeled to our planet by beings who claimed to be the Gods of their particular worlds in space. The actual person who received this knowledge while in an altered state of consciousness was never generally known because they did not attempt to gain fame or notoriety by associating themselves publicly with this material. They realized fully well that to do so would attract more attention to themselves then they either desired or deserved. Obviously, they felt that the messages they were acting as a space channel for were the important things and not the earthly messenger they came through who, after all, was only acting as a scribe.

While in the Yucca Valley, California home of Gabriel Green, director of the *Amalgamated Flying Saucer Clubs of America* (and one time space-age candidate for the office of the president of the United States), I happened to mention my plans to reprint these channeled messages under one title as I felt it was important that they be given wide circulation and made available to those who do not have access to the assorted publications of limited circulation that are passed around amongst the members of the various groups that have sprung up over the last few decade. Gabe said he remembered the channeled messages quite well and thought he could track down the identity of the channel. Since he believed the person had since passed from this plane to another dimension he saw no reason why we couldn't now use their name as sort of a tribute to their contribution to the New Age that they unselfishly refused to accept credit for while they were still living.

The person responsible for the material presented in this book is Adelaide J. Brown, who, before passing away, was one of the guiding lights of the New Age in the Los Angeles area. After reading the **SPACE GODS SPEAK**, I think you will agree that she is greatly missed upon the scene.

One thing that becomes obvious upon reading this book is that the Space Gods are speaking to all of us and they chose to speak in non-technical terms, using language that is accessible to us all regardless of our educational background. This is not a technical book, but an inspiration work meant to lift our vibrations with useful information. It is not scientific, but deeply spiritual. It has a meaning and impact that is destined to be felt more strongly by those who feel they are in service to humanity.

And it is a good thing that we have clarified elsewhere that we are primarily dealing with spiritual beings and not flesh and blood types, though does also come to visit, but certainly not from the planets in our solar system which are too hot or too cold to harbor physical bodies that resemble us doggedly human Earthlings.

One final word, the artwork in this book has been added by our lovely Carol Ann Rodriguez and is based upon her own sensitive insights as to what the Gods of these other planets look like upon those rare occasions when their vibrations are lowered and we might see them in what appears to be physical form, even if they are of a different mass or vibration.

***Timothy Green Beckley, Publisher***

- Unless otherwise specified, all art in this section Copyright © By Carol Ann Rodriguez.

Photo below by Charla Gene.

Tim Beckley looking for a ride from a friend in Sedona, Arizona

Spaceships from different planets, all members of the
Galactic Command, are visiting Earth to help humankind.

**GOD OF MARS**

# THE BOOK OF SPACE SHIPS IN THEIR RELATIONSHIP WITH THE EARTH

## By The God of a Planet Near the Earth

There has been the need for a book of this kind for some time. The world of humanity has been aroused by reports of what they at first called flying saucers, because in the sky the light struck them in such a way that they appeared to be round, like a saucer, and they were moving so fast a good view could not be had of them. More recently it has been seen that some of them are quite large and long in shape, like a ship, not round like a saucer.

But still they are mysterious objects to the inhabitants of the planet Earth, and there has been both fear and scientific interest expressed in regard to them. The answer to all questions is very simple, especially now that mankind has developed flying ships of their own. These are air ships from other planets. But the question has remained, why are they coming over the earth, are their designs sinister, or are they friendly? For a long time there was only fear expressed, because the people of Earth had become so accustomed to wars between nations, that war was the first thought in their minds. How sad this is, and entirely contrary to the truth.

Some of us have managed to contact certain members of the human race, who were of high intelligence, and whose minds were eager to know the truth and the reason for these ships of the air descending so close to the planet Earth. Some of our Space Craft have landed, and we have managed to talk with some of the more spiritually evolved members of the human race, but the vast majority of men are still worried when they hear of these ships.

It is the hope of the writer of this book, that all fear may be overcome by a presentation of the true situation by one who really knows at first hand, being a traveler in space ships, as well as an aerial traveler without any kind of vehicle but his own body. I am that kind of Being, and am the Ruler of a Planet near the earth. Every planet has a Ruler, and the name that is used for the Ruler may shock some of the devoutly religious of Earth, who do not understand. We are called Gods, and there is one for each planet.

The human race has believed for eons of time that their planet was the only one inhabited. When men looked up into the sky and saw the shining stars, the moon, and sun, they thought that all these beautiful objects were created for the benefit of the people of earth, and were comparatively small objects, as they seemed to be, to the naked eye of man. Even now when marvelous telescopes have been invented, man knows very little about the planets which appear in his telescope.

So before we enter into the subject of space ships, it is necessary to discuss planets. Space ships are used for travel between the planets, so now we shall study the planets-only those of the solar system in which the earth is a planet. Each planet is a small part of the solar system, and the solar system is only one of many solar systems, which all together make the universe. The universe is only one of many universes, which all together are beyond the imagining of the mind of man.

Close your eyes, relax, and try to imagine anything extending in all directions without any ending. This is the universe of universes. How small and insignificant is a solar system in comparison, and how extremely small is one planet of a solar system, What we are now concerning ourselves with, is the planet Earth and its sister planets.

All the planets are globes, as is the earth, but the globes vary greatly in size: There are many which are very much larger than the little planet Earth. Mars, Jupiter, Venus, to mention a few. Astronomers, at the present time, are learning much about the planets that they never knew before, but it is still comparatively little. The distances between the planets is not very great, and can be easily traveled by space ships, which are very much more advanced inventions than the airplanes of the earth. They are noiseless, and their power is derived from the atmosphere, and is pure and without odor.

For centuries man has believed his Earth to be the only inhabited planet. Certain conditions of warmth, moisture, soil, etc., were considered necessary for the life of any being resembling man or animal. He has made two mistakes. In the first place, all living creatures do not need the same conditions that man does; in the second place, man's scientific instruments do not accurately register the conditions that prevail on each planet.

The truth is that almost every planet is inhabited by beings very similar to man. There also is vegetable and animal life. In fact, few of the planets are barren and uninhabitable.

Besides this, many of them have civilizations which far surpass that of any nation on the earth. It is known by your historians that there have been civilizations on earth that have fallen and disappeared. Archaeologists are now making discoveries which show that there were marvelously advanced civilizations on the earth, which for one reason or another; were destroyed, and disappeared from the face of the earth. Their marvelous cities are being uncovered, and much is being learned about the lives of those ancient peoples.

Wonderful civilizations like these are now flourishing on many of the planets in this solar system. There are some more backward than the Earth, but they are few. The majority are equal to the Earth, or in advance of it. Man has begun to question, "Why should the Earth be the only inhabited planet?" The answer is, it is not.

Now man is endeavoring to obtain information concerning the planet Mars and the moon. There is much talk about the atmosphere of the moon, and the soil. Some scientists say the soil is only dry dust, which is blown about by the wind. Others contradict this and say it is rich and could be productive. All study is for the purpose of using the moon as a defense base from which to hurl bombs on the enemy. How sad this is! Instead of living together in peace, harmony and brotherly love, the human race, in all parts of the Earth, is either fighting with physical weapons, or competing with one another for the gaining of wealth and luxury. It is all fighting and war though different kinds.

How different it is on the planets in the neighborhood of the Earth, those of whose inhabitants the Earth people are so much afraid. They judge only by themselves, and therefore believe the inhabitants of these planets to be warlike and greedy, as they are. So when occasionally a space ship is seen, it is assumed that its purpose is to harm the inhabitants of earth.

This writing is for the purpose of dispelling this erroneous idea. We are reaching out the hand of friendship and man believes it is holding a bomb. Instead of this it is an offer of information and assistance in the building of space craft, for ours are far in advance of the noisy, clumsy, flying ships of the planet Earth. The few understanding ones of Earth would be pleased to have our cooperation and would pass our information to the others who are of a scientific turn of mind.

The first thing is to learn how to use the energy that is in the atmosphere. This runs our ships and is always available without cost. The next thing is to learn to make the craft a somewhat different shape than the present airplanes. The present planes are beautiful as they fly high in the air looking like great dragon flies sailing with spread wings, but the shape of our ships is much more practical for the purpose for which they are used-flight.

But the very first thing to accomplish is to overcome man's suspicious attitude and win the trust and friendship of humanity.

This must be done by spiritual teaching, and the knowledge of our philosophy, which is more than philosophy to discuss and exercise the mind on, it is the breath of life to us and we practice and live it. I shall now explain this knowledge.

It is very much like the New Age teaching of the earth. This New Age teaching is Truth, but only a comparatively small number of the people study it, and not all of them practice it. We believe with all our hearts that there is a Mighty Power, invisible to all eyes, which is the cause of all life and the sustainer of it.

We do not give It the name of God, we call It Life Eternal. We feel Its Presence all around us, in us and acting through us. I am one of those we call Gods. We are very advanced in the art of living. We are able to perform miracles, as you call them. These are all natural phenomena. We who are Gods do not need space ships for our travels, we can move rapidly through space by psychic forces that are in our bodies. And we do not need to move in order to see, hear and know all that takes place everywhere.

Each planet has a God who has created the planet. It is so of the Earth. You people of Earth have a wonderful God who has created the planet Earth He loves all His creation just as we all do. It has been said, God is Love and that is true of all Gods. All the planets near the earth have Gods of love and the inhabitants of the planets in turn love their Gods with all their hearts, minds and strength.

It would be impossible for the people of these planets to deliberately injure any living being. They all live lives of love and joy, for true love is joy. No one who feels that love and joy could ever hurt another living thing. This is what we are trying to make man understand.

If mankind would drop their destructive ways, they too would live lives of love and joy, without conflict of any kind. All would be peace and plenty.

Oh, if man would only understand and he shall understand after reading this book and others, which shall tell of the experiences of enlightened men, who have seen the space ships and talked with those who came to Earth in them. These illumined ones have had great trouble in making their fellow men believe their reports of their experiences. Man is notably reluctant to accept any new belief or idea, he clings tenaciously to his old established beliefs and practices.

But this shall soon change, for the pressure of Truth is becoming too great to be resisted. It is not very long now, as time is measured, before mankind will accept the fact that there are other inhabited planets, and the fact that the inhabitants of those planets near the Earth not only can visit the Earth, but are visiting the Earth. More persons will be seeing the space craft and, as the old human saying goes, "seeing is believing."

That has been the great trouble with humanity; they have put greater reliance on their physical eyes than on their mental understanding. It is well known that the report of the eyes cannot be accepted as it seems to be. A trite example is, the railroad tracks do not come closer together in the distance. Investigation and knowledge has proven that fact. Investigation and knowledge must be applied to every new experience, no matter what it may be, whether pleasant and desirable or unpleasant. The truth should be searched for and when found accepted. Turning the back and looking away from a fact, will not change or remove it.

Enough persons have encountered space ships from other planets and talked with those in them to make it an established fact. Now the next thing to do is to investigate and find out what and who they are, and why they are visiting the planet Earth. This writing is a simple and frank presentation of the truth of the situation, but man must investigate with an open mind and find the truth of the matter for himself.

The question is...how can this be done? It is simple to answer. Most of the ships have been appearing in the United States of America, for this is the country most able to follow directions in building these craft. It will require money and skilled scientists to build them. The method of drawing the power from the atmosphere is not difficult, but it requires scientific minds to understand it. There are plenty of such minds in this great country. But there are not so many minds that are without prejudice.

It is strange, but it is a fact, that brilliant and well educated scientists are among the slowest people to accept a new thought or idea. It is a rule with them to accept no new concept until it has been proven. But how can it be proven, if it is shut out without investigation just because it is new? How strangely the minds of even the most intelligent men can act. It is said that Diogenes went about with a lantern searching for an honest man. So we might search for an unprejudiced man. It is indeed rare to find any member of the human race, man, woman or child entirely without prejudice. However we do find some who will listen to reason, and who can be persuaded to finally accept new concepts. It is our hope that one scientist may be found, who is intelligent to a high degree and without strong prejudice. We have faith that this shall be.

Besides these two qualifications there is a third that is necessary; he must be able to receive instruction spiritually by telepathy. That is the way this writing is being done; some call it dictation in the mind. The communication between giver and receiver is very close. It is often so close that the one receiving believes he is thinking, and the words are his own. He has no knowledge that another mind from another dimension of life is speaking into his mind.

Man calls this inspiration. Musicians and painters are inspired in this way, by impressions received from higher dimensions, which are above the ordinary man's understanding. This communication is very easy between planets of this solar system. We feel sure that we shall find a scientist of this type whom we can inspire in the invention of a space ship similar to ours. It will be new to him, but it will not be really new.

All originates in the One Great Source, which is expressing everywhere, in everything. This Great Source is Life, and from It flows Life in every expression. We who are called Gods are expressions of Life, which flows from the One Great Source, and takes form.

I shall give myself as an example. I created this planet and breathed the breath of Life into all the inhabitants, whom I also formed. But the power and ability to do this were not mine; I received the power and knowledge from the One Great Source. This is what Jesus meant when he said, "Of myself I can do nothing, it is the Father within me who doeth the works."

That is the truth of all Life in one sentence. I say the same of myself, for acting in and through me is a higher Being, and above and in him is a higher Being than he, and so on back to the Great Source of all Life. All the planets, solar systems, and universes were created in this way. You who are reading this were created in this way. Nothing was created in any other way. Life originated in the One Great Source, which had no beginning, and shall have no end. We cannot imagine what It is like, it is beyond our imagination. We only know that It is, and that without It nothing would be.

The space ships were created in this way, and in this way man can create them if he so desires. For desire is a necessary step in the creation of any-thing. Without desire nothing comes into existence. Strong, steady, unwavering desire is a must in all creation. It must be without doubt. There must be a sureness of accomplishment that nothing can shake.

That is the way man has evolved and unfolded. That is the way the lower forms of life have evolved. They do not reason, they do not think as man does, but within them is an unconscious de-sire for something more. They change from a lower form to a higher, more complex form, with a higher state of consciousness. By a strong desire man can accomplish anything, for it is not he who accomplishes, but the power of the Great Source of Life that is in him, and in all that is. Without Life nothing could take form and be active.

So we of the planets near the Earth offer our assistance to the Earth, but without the desire and acceptance of man nothing can be accomplished. With desire there must be love for that which is desired. Love is the source of all creation. One must love ones work in order to be successful. All great scientists love their work. They will devote many hours, without rest or sleep, when they feel that something is being accomplished, or about to be brought to light. Those persons who work only for money are weary before the day is over.

So in order for us to give man the secret of our space craft, we must find at least one scientist of the highest caliber, who can receive that which we have to give. How joyfully we shall give instruction when it is desired. How much love we shall pour into the work along with our knowledge. Our space ships can be copied, or perhaps even improved. Who knows?

Intercourse between the Earth and the other planets is the result which will follow the construction of these ships of the air. From visits to the other planets man will see how life can be lived in brotherly love, and what joy, peace and plenty, both spiritual and physical, will result when love rules instead of force.

Oh beloved ones of the Earth, our hearts ache when we see the misery, poverty, and greed upon the Earth. All is force and struggle. With us all is peace and harmony. It is our strong desire to see the people of Earth living also in love, with plenty of material gifts for all, nature responding to the love that will fill the atmosphere. Our love we send to you, our help we offer to you, we pray it be accepted. If man could only see our beautiful planets and realize that the same beauty, joy and peace could be his on the planet Earth, he would surely make every effort to attain this Wonderful joy and peace.

It is the peace of God which passeth understanding. It is in the center of every living being, ready to come forth into the outer life. This it cannot do in the midst of hatred and selfishness. In divine love there is the peace which will revolutionize the world of man. It may seem that I repeat this too often, but repetition is necessary in order to anchor the point in the minds of mankind.

Now you have been told what to do and what not to do, the next thing is how to do it. It has been said, and rightly, that one cannot love to order, love is spontaneous. Yes, but it can be brought forth by acting in the way love calls for. Do unto others as you would have them do to you. This does not mean for the purpose of having them do the same to you. No, it is simply a gauge for action, and when this is practiced love will follow. Be honest in all your dealings, give a little more rather than a little less. This old motto means exactly what it states, there is no return promised. But there is a return after practicing this for some time; love will be felt for the ones one has dealings with, and they, subconsciously will feel that love and return it.

This is the recipe for peace on earth, goodwill toward men. You upon the earth have just celebrated the birth of your beloved Master Jesus who loves all mankind with a love that transcends all darkness, and brings the light into all hearts and minds that will open to receive it. During the time of Christmas much love flows forth from the hearts of mankind. The giving and receiving of presents is done in love and peace and little children are especially recipients of this love and joy.

Oh, if this blessed time could be al-ways, what a different place the Earth would be. Peace would replace battle, love would replace selfish greed. This is what the other planets wish to help the Earth people to attain and keep. There is some love now, and the problem is to expand it, to make it flow out in all directions with depth and sincerity.

We believe that visits to her sister planets; tours of inspection; conversations with the inhabitants; visits of a week or more in order to make friends; would open the eyes, hearts and minds of the inhabitants of Earth so that they would desire to follow our example.

Desire is the first step in any accomplishment. A strong, eager desire will be followed by an effort to learn how to attain that which is desired. This will be followed by action. With love in the heart for the Great Source of all Life, Love and Peace from which all blessings flow, humanity will become one with the similar beings on the other planets in this solar system.

There are many more solar systems, but love begins at home and from there goes out to other systems beyond us. As I have said before, much depends upon your scientists. Most of you will be astonished to hear that already there are scientists on the earth who are receiving instruction from our planet – the one on which I dwell. They do not yet know that what comes to them as inspiration is coming from scientists of another planet.

Some of the more spiritually minded ones realize that they are in communication with a higher source, but they do not know that the source is another planet. They will be informed of this soon now, for everything on the earth is being speeded up. The spiritual atmosphere is being purified and the light is beginning to drive out the darkness. There will soon be a great upheaval all over the planet Earth. This is unavoidable.

In order to let the good come in the evil must be driven out, the two cannot exist together. Selfishness must disappear and love can then enter in. But, and this seems strange and contradictory, the cleansing must be done with love. The vigorous action hurts and destroys, but the vigorous action of cleansing comes from pure, divine love. This is beginning on the earth now and will continue for some time, growing stronger and more painful.

The dwellers on my planet are not taking any part in the cleansing; this is, as you might say "none of our business." Our work is to help in the reconstruction that will follow the cleansing, and as has been already stated, we are now inspiring, helping, and informing those spiritually able to receive our communications.

This book is one of our means of communication. It is intended to reach many thousands of people, who are ready to receive information if it is simply and clearly stated, and above all, honest. This book is all of that and we know that it will receive a hearty welcome.

My love and blessing is in every word; the love and blessing of the one who writes is in every word; and the love and blessing of all my people is in every word; for they know that this is being written. Those who read it will feel that love, even though it may be unconsciously, and it will give them understanding and warm their hearts.

So, as you read, you are receiving benefit both mentally and physically, for my vibrations are flowing from the atmosphere around this book all through your being. The publishers and the printer also have received these vibrations, and have added to them their own, which are high. This is true of all spiritual books, but few persons know this.

What marvelous times are coming after the cleansing period is over on your dear planet Earth. After the cleansing period, which will be a time of great suffering and anguish, the skies will clear, the Sun Righteousness will shine over all the Earth and the Great God of Earth will reign supreme. Every human being will feel the Life and Love from the Great Source of Being active within his human form. The Christ Self will speak and act in everyone.

But since man has been given free will up to a certain point, the time of the coming of this release from misery and entrance into pure joy depends on man himself. His mind must be cleared of misconceptions and his heart must be filled with love. We of the planets near the Earth can help him to replace the misconceptions with Truth, and that will bring love into his heart.

The first step to take is to let all the inhabitants of Earth know who we are and why we are visiting the Earth in our space ships. Some already know this and are heart and soul desirous of receiving us and hearing what we have to tell them. This is a focal point from which the knowledge will spread in all directions. It is already spreading. Groups of people on the Earth have come together for the sole purpose of making contact with our ships and receiving the message of those on them. This has been accomplished by means of tape recorders. Before this there were instances of ships landing on the Earth and communication being made with individuals who were open minded and eager to receive them. Books were written and something was accomplished in arousing interest, but it did not spread far enough or fast enough. Something more had to be done and now is being done.

We have been able to go close to the Earth and our messages are received on tape recorders. These tapes can be mailed to great distances; other tapes can be made from them and sent out in other directions, and so the information is really spreading.

Now the doubters have raised a question that is a very reasonable one. How can those from other planets speak the language of the people they contact, without foreign accent, as easily and smoothly as a native. Surely they do not all speak English on the other planets. These tapes must be made by words spoken by dishonest individuals on the earth.

This is a reasonable question and the answer is simple. We on the other planets do not have to learn a new language word for word as you do on Earth. Even you Earth people have some persons who have what are called photographic memories. They remember what they have read, a whole page at a time, not by hearing but by sight. When they return home from a sightseeing trip of week's duration they remember it all as pictures in their mind, unfolding one after another in sequence. Musicians remember the printed notes and the sounds of whole symphonies; singers remember both words and music. Your babies do not come into the world talking, they learn by listening to the adults and older children around them.

Now you understand how we are able to speak your languages without difficulty. We come close enough so that we can hear you talk. We are often invisible to your human eyes, and we can hear and see you. It is necessary, in order to communicate with you, that we should be able to speak your language. So, to meet the necessity, we learn your language. It is easy for us for we have what you would call phenomenal memories. We never forget anything that we wish to remember.

You people of earth can learn to do all of these things for already some of you can do them. But the one great and important thing that we want you to do is to learn to send out impersonal Divine love. On the planets near the Earth we do that and it has become second nature to us. Instead of using force to accomplish our desires we send out love, which is the greatest power in the universe. When we desire to build a city, for instance, all those engaged in the project, before they begin, send thoughts of pure love to one another and keep those thoughts sustained throughout the whole time of planning and construction. This causes everything to move so smoothly that it seems as if the city almost builds itself.

If there is disagreement it is settled by quiet, reasonable discussion and soon the best plan is followed. This is only an example of the power of love. In quarreling and trying to force your opponents to adopt your way, confusion exists and much time and effort is taken to accomplish that which should be easily done.

Life is Love, Love is Life, and Life and God are one and the same. Life is everywhere, in everything, for it is existence. In the depths of creation Love reigns supreme, though on the surface it may seem to be lacking. The reader may think that we have left the subject of space ships, but this is still on the subject. That is the way our space ships are built-with love. The ideas for the invention of these very successful "birds of the air," as we lovingly call them, all came to us in love, never in bickering or dislike of any one. All great inventors have loved their inventions and those for whom the inventions were made.

Love is the explanation of our visits to the planet Earth. That is the only reason for our coming. We can see the terrible turmoil and confusion on the Earth caused by man's mistaken idea that force rules and overcomes all that is wrong. This is far from the truth, for force itself is entirely wrong. Nothing lasting has ever been accomplished by force. We have learned that by thinking and reasoning, for we are reasonable beings. Man is supposed to be a reasonable being but the fact is that he is not. He is governed by his emotions almost entirely. Emotions cause prejudice and prejudices cause emotions. Of course there are good emotions, and love is one of these and the most powerful. But in order to be powerful it must be pure, Divine love, not the possessive emotion that is sometimes, in fact often, called love.

The love that I am speaking of is entirely unselfish. It is the pure Love of God which will flow through any human heart if it is open and unobstructed by wrong mental images. You may not think that we are human, but we are very like you, we have minds to think and hearts to love, and we use them to good purpose.

You have minds and hearts but it seems to us who watch you that you do not use either. You must learn to use both mind and heart if you wish to untangle the mess that you are in. We love you as we love every living being, and again I say we are ready to help you in any way we can. The first way would probably be to teach you to build really good space ships. Yours are noisy and they pollute the air with harmful smokes and gases. We fly without noise or smoke. After you have built some like ours you will be able easily to visit our planets as well as the moon. But not for purposes of war, but as friendly visitors desiring to understand the lives of their neighbors. The time is past when the little earth was seemingly a large globe, and travel from one place to another was on foot or horseback or in horse drawn vehicles. Now distances are short on the surface of the Earth and also short between the Earth and other planets. Perhaps I have repeated this too often, but I hope to make it sink into the minds and hearts of those who read. Then they will spread the truth among their friends and acquaintances with good results. Education is what is needed at this time.

Education is the purpose of this book. There is not much to say but what is said is right to the point and means a great deal. After this assurance of our friendship, you who dwell on the Earth will have no fear when we visit your planet. Since we speak your language fluently, we will be able to plan together how to educate the mass of people on Earth so that they may desire peaceful living without conflict of any kind, either physical or mental.

This book is easy to read and is only an opening wedge, so to speak. It is a forerunner of more erudite ones to follow. Those which follow will be books of science and will be concerned with the building and operating of space craft.

The dictation of these will be from scientists to scientists.

With these words I bid you farewell. My love and blessing is with you in all your endeavors. My name would mean nothing to you, but those who are sensitive will feel my love and blessing.

**All originates in the One Great Source. This Great Source is Life, and we who are called Gods are expressions of Life, which flows from the One Great Source, and takes form.**

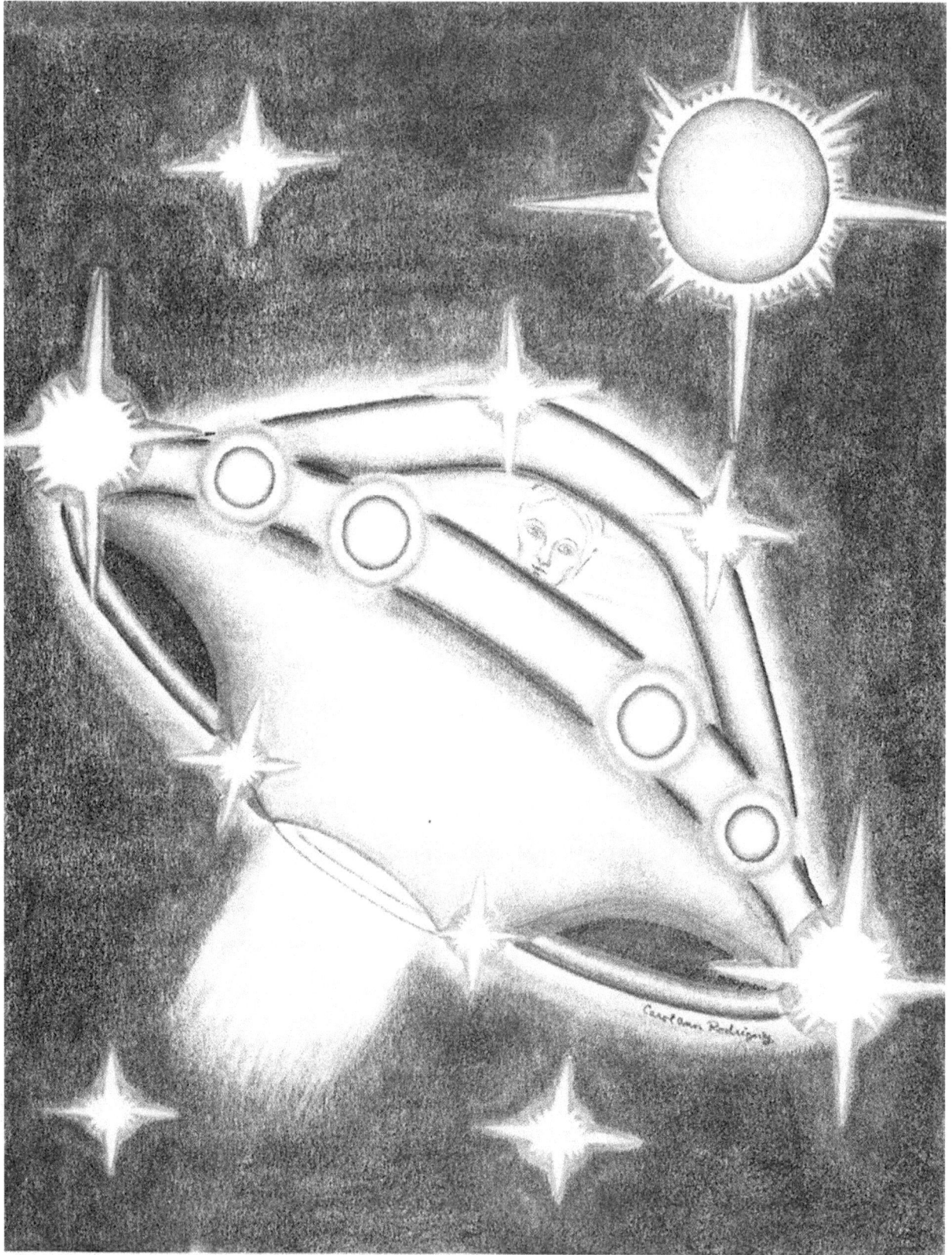

**GOD OF PLUTO**

# FROM PLANET PLUTO WITH BROTHERLY LOVE

**T**he inhabitants of the Planet Pluto are very similar to those of the Earth. Our bodies are like yours in every respect. Our height is like yours, being different with each individual. Some tall, some short, some medium in height. Indeed, I think the Planet Pluto resembles the Earth more closely than any of the other planets, except in one important respect – we live in peace and brotherly love.

There are no wars, no quarrels, no crimes, such as robbery, murder etc. The Earth is the only planet in this solar system which is not peaceful and happy. This seems very strange, and surely something could be done to eliminate this condition and bring peace and happiness to the Earth.

There are many loving Earth people now who are devoting themselves to works of charity. There are many organizations active in helping the needy and the sick. There are free schools and colleges for the education of the youth of the land. When we see all this which is beautiful, we wonder how there can be the ruthless competition in business, and the wars which are always being waged on some part of the Earth.

Has there ever been a time when peace prevailed over the entire surface of the globe? There has never been such a time.

Why? We who are looking on ask, why? It is said that there is always a reason for everything, so there must be a reason for this sad state of affairs. We must look and see if we can find the cause.

In what way does the Earth differ from the other planets, which never have wars? The cause may perhaps be found in the number of nationalities, which are different in language and appearance. One nation cannot understand the language of another without study in school. Customs and habits of everyday life also differ.

In early times there were continual wars between peoples of different countries for the purpose of carrying away spoil. The soldiers returned from the war laden with riches taken from the enemy, and driving before them slaves which were made from the captives of war.

There was usually no good reason for the war. One country accused the other of stepping over the boundary line, perhaps. But usually there was only the difference in language and the desire for spoil.

At one time the Roman Empire owned most of the Earth. At another time Spain became most powerful. The tiny country of England once bragged that "the sun never sets on British possessions."

At this very moment wars are being fought and young men are being drafted into the army, taken from their homes to fight for they know not what.

This has been the history of the Planet Earth. A sad history it has been. A record of bloodshed and robbery. We shall try to find the reason for this and try to find a remedy.

The reason seems to be a strong feeling of separation between nations and a strong desire for the acquiring of riches by any means. When we look closer we see that the riches were enjoyed by a very small number of the population – by those in power as rulers and their associates. The great majority of the people received little benefit.

What was lacking on the Earth that we of the other planets possessed? The lacking quality was love for God. With love for God, the Father of all, love for man would follow.

In very early times, the Israelites considered themselves the chosen people of God. All others were aliens. But these people did not love their God as a Heavenly Father; they feared Him as a mighty King. They were the chosen people of this mighty King and all others were their enemies. There was no love in their religion. In the Old Testament it is stated, "The Lord Thy God is a jealous God." Never was He a loving Father.

This was changed with the advent of Jesus, the Christ, whose teaching was love. Love for God the Father and love for their brother men was the teaching preached and emphasized. His disciples lived and preached this teaching and they had many followers. But, alas, as time moved on, there were differences of opinion among his followers, arguments over trivial matters of ritual. Instead of one church, there were many, and one which gained power would persecute the others.

So the beautiful teaching of love for God and for all humanity received only lip service; it did not penetrate into the hearts of the majority. There were saints who lived the teaching, but they were a very small minority. War and bloodshed did not cease, only the cause was different. One religion would be in power and all others must be crushed. Where was the beautiful teaching of love for God and man?

Once more the rich in worldly goods were in power, acting under the pretense of religion. You see, we on Pluto have watched the Earth, for we have been able to see that which was taking place just as easily as one country could follow events in another. More easily than the primitive countries with their lack of transportation could.

We of Pluto can read minds, as some of mankind can do, but with us it is universal. In the minds of the people of Earth we saw the reason for their greed and cruelty. Their thoughts were almost always busy with self. The mothers of families were the only ones with unselfish love for others; they would sacrifice their own comfort for the welfare of their little ones. We looked into the minds of the fathers and found that many of them also loved their children devotedly and some husbands and wives truly loved each other unselfishly.

But beyond this love did not go. There was no love for the neighbors or for God Almighty. There was suspicion for the neighbors and fear for God. How different it was on Pluto. Our love flowed forth to all those around us, and rose to our Heavenly Father with devotion and joy.

With true love comes joy and peace. When a whole population loves, they live in joy and peace. There cannot be war and destruction. There cannot be cheating and trickery. Now we have found the cause of all the unhappiness on Earth: It is caused by lack of love for God and their brother man. What about the religions of Earth, is there not love in them? Yes, in the religions love can be found, but there is much fear mixed with love for God, and love for each other does not go beyond those who practice the same religion, the same ceremonies, and the same dogmas. There have been terrible wars waged in the name of religion. Much cruelty – even torture – has been practiced in the name of religion, even in the same nation.

The Crusades of the Middle Ages were wars waged by the Christians against the Moslems in the name of Christ Jesus. Love was forgotten and cruelty reigned supreme. This is only one example of how the followers of a religion which taught love completely ignored that teaching.

If it were understood and realized that there is one Source of all life, one Source only, then humanity would be brought together in peace and love. If the

Source were loved and worshipped by all, and it were understood that all life proceeded from that source, then the realization of brotherhood would follow. We of Pluto have understood this and felt and practiced this love for many centuries, more than we can count. We do not remember a time when we did not love and worship the One Great Source of all Life. We realize that we all have come forth from the One Great Source of Life and we know in our minds and hearts that we all are the One in expression. All are the One Life in manifestation.

Then how could one of us hurt another? How could there be wars, greed and hatred? These could not be for we know – really know – that we are all One, being parts of the One Great Life from which all that is comes forth. All the planets know this except the planet Earth. Why is this so? Why do not the people of Earth know in the depths of their beings that all are one – all children of the One Great Father? Why do they not know that, when they injure their brother, they are injuring themselves? For all life is One Life, there is no separation.

The Earth has never been without great teachers who have preached and prophesied, urging their hearers to worship their God and love one another. They had followers who listened to their words, but very few took their teaching into their hearts and lived it. But I am thankful that I can say that at the present time there is a glimmer of hope that this denseness will be penetrated by the Light which never fails.

In many parts of the Earth people have come together in groups and listen to the words of illumined ones who live and understand. Many of these groups have been formed in the United States of America. They all teach love and unity. The Light is spreading in all directions and hearts are filling with love. But still there are wars raging upon the Earth. It seems that war has become a habit, the only way that is known to settle a dispute. How stupid this is! Yes, stupid is the only word for it. How strange that people who are otherwise intelligent should still cling to the practice of war, with all the misery and suffering that it causes.

You who read these words can help to do away with war. How can an individual in private life do anything to prevent war? By prayer to God Almighty. And He is not far off in the sky but within you, and within all that lives. For God and Life are the same. "The prayer of a righteous man availeth much." So no one is helpless, anyone can pray with a heart full of love for God and humanity. Pray more than twice a day. At any time, in any place, your thought can fly forth carrying love and supplication, with faith that the prayer shall be answered. Some groups use decrees, which are very good. There is no hard and fast rule for communicating with the Father within. Desire and love with faith are all that is needed.

If the desire for peace on Earth is strong, a habit is soon formed to send out prayers or decrees very frequently without pausing in whatever you may be doing. The hands may be busy, but thought is free to rise to any height. "Peace on Earth, goodwill toward men" the angels sang when Jesus the Christ was born. We on the Planet Pluto heard the wonderful chorus and know that this is true.

There is much skepticism on the planet Earth. It is thought by many that much of the beautiful teaching in the Bible is false, only stories or parables to express spiritual teaching. True, there are parables given as such, but the so-called miracles were true and the same could be performed now if mankind had faith and enough love. "Ask and it shall be given unto you." But there must be no doubt in the asking. Asking with doubt in the mind is no better than not asking at all. Also, when decrees are given, they must be given with faith that that which they demand is an accomplished fact. They must be given with love and faith in God and love and faith in man.

This, is being taught by many organizations on the Earth today and many hundreds of people are practicing this. It is a practice for individuals in their homes at any time of the day or night. Calamities have been averted by this means. Great earthquakes, tidal waves, storms of thunder and lightning, have been controlled and either eliminated or made very much less severe. Predictions have failed to come to pass and many persons have believed that the prophets were mistaken. Only those who have been sending forth the prayers and decrees have known why the predicted calamity did not come as had been predicted.

Wonderful is the love of God for man.

Every opportunity is given humanity to reform, change their ways of greed and battle, for ways of love and peace. We other planets were inspired by God to offer our assistance and to tell of our own ways of living in peace and love. We are all very happy to do anything we can to help. By means of these little booklets we introduce ourselves and offer our friendship.

There has always been friendship and free communication between all the planets in this solar system, with the exception of the Planet Earth. The inhabitants of that planet have held aloof. Many years ago it was believed that the Earth was flat and, if one travelled too far, he would fall off the edge. In the mind of man the Earth was all. There was no other life.

Now, by means of powerful instruments and life-long study by those called astronomers, the fact has been discovered that the Earth and all other planets are globes, not flat surfaces. From the Earth astronauts are now being sent up in specially constructed ships – we would call them – to explore the spheres around the Earth. We are watching with interest, and if they should land we would greet them cordially.

It is very possible that the astronauts may be able to land on one of the planets or on the moon. They are learning much about travel in the higher realms above the planet Earth. If they do land, they will find much to interest them. The large population, the towns and cities, the trees and flowers, all so much like the Earth. We can read minds and we can speak any language, so there will be no obstacle in the way of communication. How happy we shall be if one day we see them land.

Our little children will run forth to greet them, for the little ones are much interested in what they have been told about life and living, and their minds and hearts are open and receptive to new experiences. They know that there is one God, Creator of all that is; they know that God is Love and they are afraid of nothing. They are like the little children of Earth in their innocence and activity.

It is the same on all the planets. No matter where the astronauts may land they will be cordially greeted.

Everywhere is life and life and God are One...the only One that is. We know that we are all brothers, children of the one Father. Our lives are lived in love and peace, for we truly know in the depths of our beings that all life is one life, there is no separation.

This is being taught now in many places on the Planet Earth. When we come close to the Earth we can hear what is being said. Walls do not shut us out; we can pass through them with ease. We do not go with idle curiosity but with love and a desire to be of help.

We are pleased to hear the true teaching being given in many groups. By far the greatest number of them are in the United States of America. Next in number are the other English-speaking peoples.

The knowledge that life and God are one and that all is God, there is no separation, is doing much to bring peace and love among nations. In God we live and move and have our being, and by God we live and move and have our being. For there is only one that acts and that is God. It is difficult to understand this at first, for we feel as if we were the actors. That is because the connection is so close between God and us. In fact there is no division, all is one and that One is God.

That might make it seem that we do not exist. We do exist in the mind and heart of the Creator for Creator and created are One substance and that substance is the only substance everywhere. Pure substance fills all seeming space and from it all is formed. There are no empty spaces anywhere. The human eye cannot see the shining substance, just as the human ear cannot hear the music of the planets moving in their orbits. There is a musical sound from everything that moves, and all is moving in the one shining substance that is everywhere. Highly illumined ones see and feel and hear, but the vast majority of mankind are oblivious to the beauty in which they live.

We of the Planet Pluto learned the truth of life many eons ago and we have never forgotten. The joy of living in this realization is very great, and it is our strong desire that our brothers of the Earth shall attain this realization and live in this joy. Our prayers go out to the One Great Source of all being, in whom all is, was, and ever shall be. It may seem that prayers should not be needed since all is one. In life there are many seeming contradictions, which are really not contradictions to a loving heart and a clear mind. All creation is governed by law – Divine Law. These laws originate in the Source of all being. There is a law that the created shall love and worship the Creator. The Creator does love His creation. When the created ones do their part in loving and worshipping the Creator, all is truly one and that One is God.

So prayers are needed from all creation. The birds and animals unconsciously send forth love in their feelings of joy and life. They live their lives by instinct, they do not reason, they feel and act as they are moved to act. The higher forms of creation have been given the power to think and reason. On the Planet Earth this power has been neglected...and instead of pure reason...the emotions of liking and disliking have been lived by to a great extent. This has been the cause of many wars. If the rulers of the nations would come together and discuss their problems with reason and love for each other, instead of unreasonable dislike, many wars would be prevented.

This would not be difficult. Man has caused all his troubles and agony by lack of love. In the private lives of the people only their own family and some friends are loved. This is not the way to live. There should be love for all the population whether seen or unseen, whether congenial or not.

This is the way of life on Pluto. It has always been the way of life and we are very happy people. All differences of opinion are discussed with reason. Each is carefully considered and finally the most reasonable action is pursued. This is not difficult to do because there is no egotism, no selfishness, and love reigns supreme.

That is the way our planet is ruled, entirely by reason, and, I should add, by love. Hatred is unknown. Dear people of Earth, you could do this, for you are not on the whole stupid or lacking in intelligence. Those in important positions are intelligent, but many are lacking in pure love for all creation. Only their own country is loved and other countries are beyond the pale, as it were.

For happy peaceful living there must be love for all, not for a selected few. How cold and lifeless this seems, although love for a few is better than no love at all. There are individuals who love no one but themselves and the feeling for themselves is not love but greed.

But in the darkness there is a glimmer of light. Many groups have been formed on the Earth for the purpose of studying the truth of living, and these are sending out much love and light to all humanity. They are devoted people, devoted to the service of God and humanity. They unselfishly give much time to sending forth love, and love and light are one.

This is not done yet in all the countries of the Earth, but it is spreading among the English-speaking people, and, like a great fire, it will eventually spread into all civilized countries, and from there what should stop it?

When we of Pluto discovered these beautiful groups, with their earnestness and high understanding, our hearts thrilled with joy and our love poured out to mingle with theirs. So this message from Pluto ends on a note of strong encouragement. Our love goes out to you of the Planet Earth, and we hope that the time will come when we may visit you and you may visit us, and instead of writing we may converse together.

So we bid you farewell until that happy day.

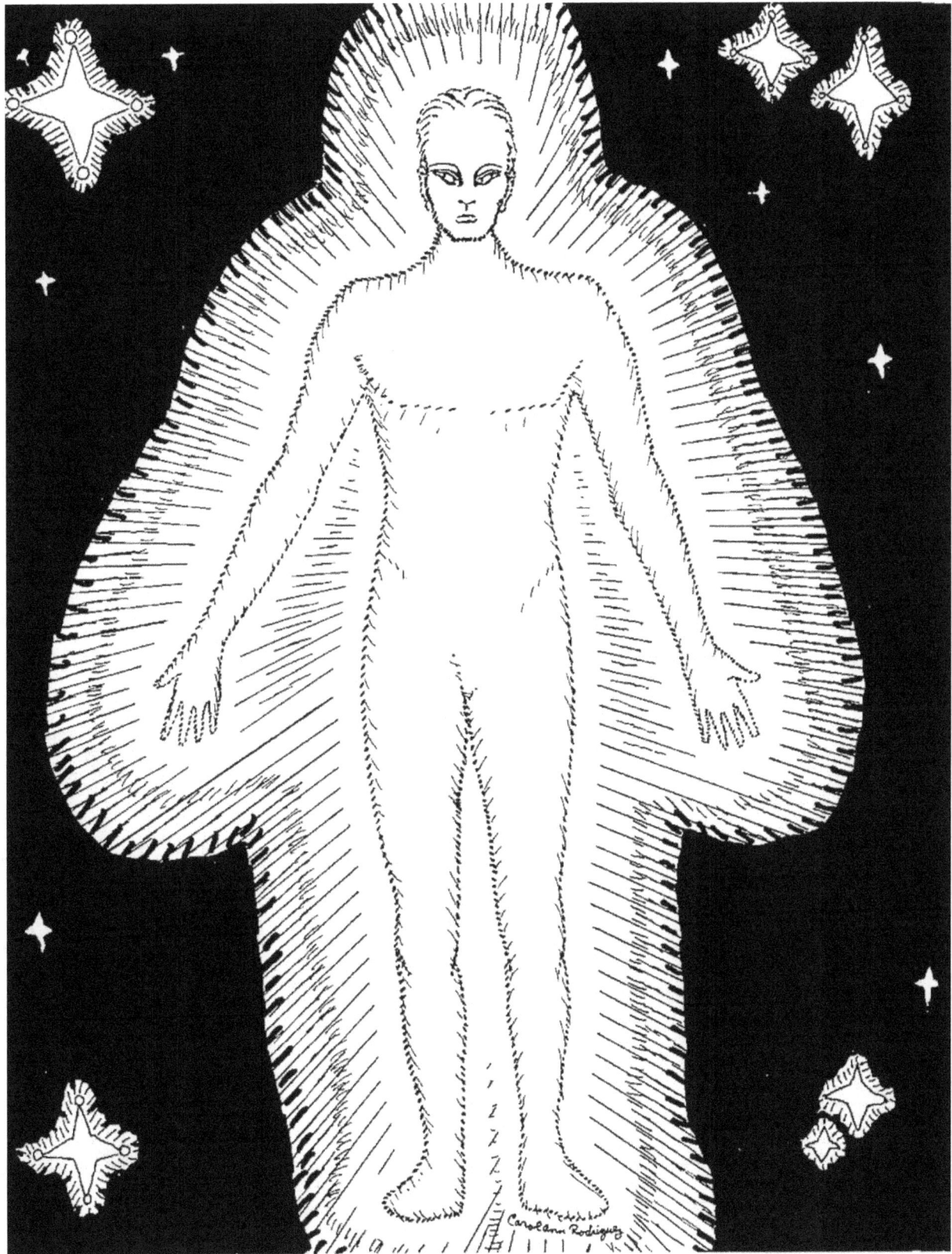

## "THE ETHERIAN"

**GOD OF NEPTUNE**

## NEPTUNE, FROM EXPERIENCE, GIVES ADVICE

**T**his is the seventh writing from the planets of the solar system of which the planet Earth is a part. It is Neptune speaking.

This writing is following close after that of Saturn, for the planets in conference had agreed that Saturn should inform mankind of the very serious situation on the Earth and close around it. Beloved Saturn accepted that unpleasant duty and performed it well. He exposed the machinations of certain beings in human form called Watchers or Money Changers. He also spoke of the dark forces hovering close to the Earth and even descending onto the Earth, and certain ones entering into the inner consciousness of individuals who were open to them because of selfishness, greed and lack of love for God, the source of all life.

Saturn performed his task, and I was called on to follow close after him because the planet Neptune had been attacked by these dark forces and had conquered and driven them away. They fled before the light that we poured forth and have never dared to return. Darkness disappears in the Light of God.

It is my duty to tell you about the experience of the population of Neptune so that the people of Earth can follow our example as quickly as possible, for the longer these dark forces are ignored, the stronger they become, drawing to them others like unto themselves.

It was many years ago that the beautiful planet Neptune became a prey of these hideous forces. With us, also, they were preceded by the beings which seemed to be physical beings like ourselves. Apparently prosperous businessmen, the same as many others. As Saturn said, they were like vampire bats sucking the blood of the planet.

When we came close to the Earth and saw these manipulators of the money system and saw behind them the black pall descending very close to the Earth, we knew from experience what it was and we planned to inform the Earth of our experience. We were in a very serious condition, but thanks be to God, we got completely rid of the Watchers and their following dark forces.

You of the Earth can do likewise when you understand what is taking place on and around your planet. So this writing will be devoted entirely to telling of our experience. We would like to tell you about our present life on our beautiful planet, but I cannot enter into that, for the most important thing is to give you the information that will help you get rid of these vampires and their following dark forces.

First it was necessary to tell you that this situation existed, and Saturn has done that. Next I will give you an account of how we of Neptune cleared our atmosphere of the darkness after getting rid of the fiends who posed as our brothers.

To look at them they appeared to be no different from any of our prosperous business men, but they were dominated by greed and were without scruple in the method of obtaining wealth. Their hearts were utterly without love. There was no feeling of sympathy for those in need; all their thought was on themselves and the amassing of riches. When we look at the Earth we see similar ones very active. These are all in private life, they hold no official positions. Your government does not know who they are or what they are.

It was the same with us; it was a long time before we knew them for what they were, and after we did know them we had to find a plan to get rid of them. You of the Earth are in the same position. Some of your people now have discovered these prosperous men and know what they are, but the majority of the population knows nothing of them and, if they hear about them, believe it is a ridiculous mistake.

We of Neptune see them clearly and assure you that what you have been told is truth. When we discovered them and knew them for what they were, we called meetings of all our governmental bodies to discuss the way to get rid of them. We knew that they were entirely evil and so could be conquered by the opposite, which is good. They loved the darkness and so could be driven away by the light. When the sun rises, all is light. So it was planned that many groups would be formed all over the planet, for the purpose of calling forth much light which would be directed onto these beings.

On your Earth there are now many groups of all sizes which are active in studying Truth and practicing it. So no groups would have to be called together, those that are already formed could take up the work. They could meet for the especial purpose of praying, decreeing, calling on God for help to expel the dark forces. These forces fear the light, the Light of God which never fails.

So the only thing that we can say is to have more meetings, pray more often, decree in private, at home many times a day. The darkness around your planet is very thick and much light will be needed to break through it and drive it away.

Each one of you needs to examine yourselves to be sure there is no feeling of selfishness or greed within your mind or heart, not even the smallest indication of it. Pure unselfish love is light from which the dark forces flee. They cannot enter any mind or heart which is full of pure, unselfish love.

This is what we did on the Planet Neptune. It took effect and the dark forces disappeared. Then we turned our attention on the seeming businessmen who were getting the finances of the planet into very bad shape. They were profiting by the losses of others. Poverty was the lot of the majority while the few lived in wealth and more than plenty.

This has been the condition on Earth for many centuries. There has been poverty for the majority, wealth for a very few. It had been accepted as the natural way of life. There were kind hearted people who gave alms to those in need; groups of women met to sew and make garments for the poor. Parties were given at which a price was charged and the money used to help the indigent.

In earlier times there were beggars on the street corners holding cups in which the passers-by dropped small coins. It was accepted by all to be the natural way of life.

On Neptune it had not been the natural way of life. There had been sufficient for all. Poverty was unknown and so also was extreme wealth. The people were all occupied in various ways. There were farmers, merchants, sellers of produce. There were dressmakers, tailors, fishers, etc. Every need was supplied by honest exchange of products or work.

There were writers of books; there were musicians, artists, both painters and sculptors; every occupation that was needed, there was. The planet was a happy place until the Watchers and Money Changers arrived.

They posed as businessmen and looked the part. But in reality they were aliens, we know not where from. It is the same at present on your planet Earth.

These aliens found their way onto the Earth and made it their home. They resemble the original population in looks and actions, but in thought and feeling they are far different.

After we cleared the atmosphere of the dark forces we turned our attention to these flesh and blood demons. It was more difficult to get rid of them because they seemed to be an integral part of the community. How could we distinguish them from other businessmen?

In looks they were the same, but in actions they were different. For one thing they were very pompous, very conceited and haughty. They looked down on plain people as if they were of no account. If they were watched awhile it was seen that they completely lacked sympathy with anyone who needed help or encouragement.

If you, our brothers of the Earth, look carefully, you will see the same thing. They are not normal persons. The mark of the beast is on them. If you will single them out and put your attention on them, you will be sure to catch them in some act of dishonesty.

It requires attention, unremitting attention. It will have to be done by those who are associated with them in some way. Not necessarily in a business way but in any association in daily living. Employer and servant; acquaintances in society; associates in business; they may be any one of these.

There is one trait among them all: they are all conceited and pompous, looking down on all they associate with. If they are carefully watched, they will be caught in some unlawful act for which they can be prosecuted.

So it was on Neptune, and, when we discovered the transgressors, they were prosecuted, convicted, and thrown into prison, where they spent the rest of their lives. Short sentences would be of no avail, it must be for life.

It was not easy but it was done, and what we have done you of Earth can do. Do not slacken for a moment in your attention. They are wily and full of tricks, but we conquered them, and their children fled from the planet into the far distance.

The Planet Neptune is now carefree and is a place of beauty and peace. It is our strong desire that our brothers and sisters of the planet Earth shall heed the warning of Saturn, and follow our example in getting completely free of the demons and the dark forces which follow them.

Our planet is now very beautiful and we are living in peace and love. There is never conflict of any kind. All is harmony and joy.

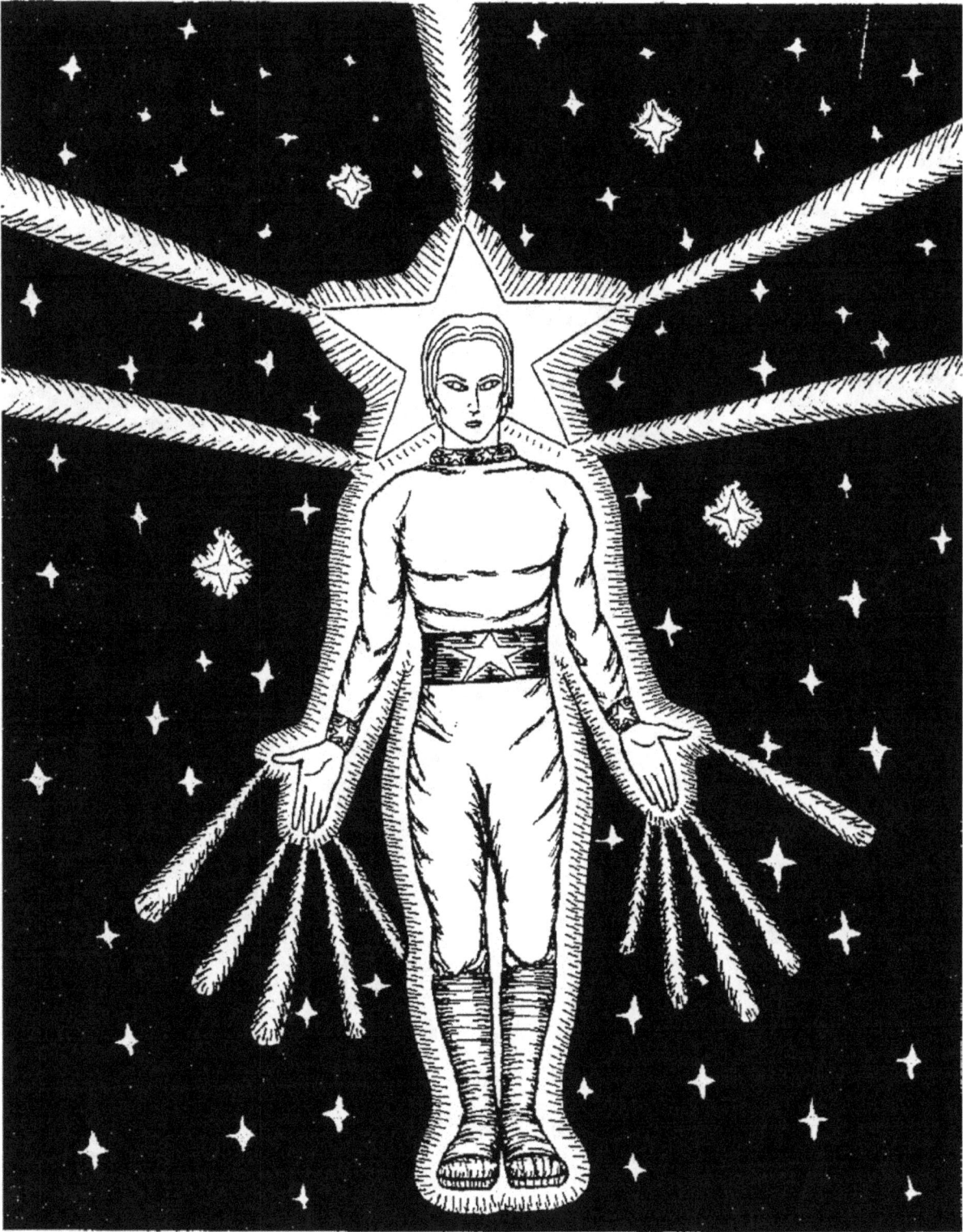

SOLAR STAR

**GOD OF URANUS**

## URANUS, LOVER OF MAN, SPEAKS

The name of this planet is Uranus. It is a large planet and much power flows from it into the atmosphere surrounding it. I who am sending this message am also called Uranus. The accent in this name is on the first syllable.

She who is taking this message felt my presence years ago and it was an experience she never forgot One day she was walking from one room to another in her house and as she opened the door a tremendous power of joy and love flowed through her being. It was so strong that she felt she might fall to the floor. She seized the doorknob and leaned against the door.

This joy and love remained strong within her for months, then gradually became less, but it has never entirely left her.

I am giving this as an example of the power which I give forth in love and joy. My action is sudden and my love is strong. This is also the disposition of my people, those who inhabit this planet.

There is no fear or hesitation on the planet Uranus. Where love and joy are present there can be no fear or hesitation.

Dear ones of Earth, we of Uranus love you and our desire is to help you to understand the meaning of Life, the joy of peace and love, the worship of the Great Life which fills all that is, making all One.

The cruelty and greed that we see on the Earth makes our hearts ache and dims our joy. Life can be so beautiful and could be so on the Earth if man could only be made to understand that Love is the great power, not force.

Almost all of the history of the Earth has been accounts of battles and blood-shed. One country fighting another in order to despoil it. In early times, enslaving the people and using them to labor in the mines and fields under the whips of overseers. Now is the age of invention so machines are used to do the work, but there is still war and bloodshed on the Earth.

We see all this from our planet, and our great desire is to see joy and love take its place. We join the other planets of this solar system in inviting mankind to visit us and experience the joy and peace of our lives.

Our flying saucers as you call them have not flown over the Earth with evil intent, but only with the desire to make friends with you, our brothers. In the first booklet of the series, the building of spaceships was urged and all the planets strongly advise this. We shall only mention this for it has been well covered in the first booklet.

We of Uranus would be pleased to have you come to our planet as our guests. I will tell you what kind of beings we are...we are of flesh, blood, bone etc., just as you are. We are not very tall, nor are we very short. We vary somewhat in height which is usually medium. We are strong and healthy, sickness is unknown, for no one who is loving and full of joy can be sick.

Just try it yourselves and see. If you stop worrying, stop complaining, stop fighting and struggling, you will never be sick. Love and joy are better than any medicine. We have heard of sickness but none of us have ever experienced it.

Another thing...we are careful not to overeat and we do not drink spirituous liquors. Being well and healthy, we do not feel the need of any stimulant; tobacco, alcohol or drugs of any kind. Our sensible way of living makes us healthy and our good health makes life joyful and radiant.

Come and see us on our planet and you will understand that which I am telling you. Eons ago we were not like this. We forgot the Great Source of life, and worry and struggle took possession of us. We were then very much as you are now. But a great Teacher arose in our midst. He spoke eloquently and with conviction and persuasion.

Some of us listened to him and followed in his steps. Others saw the benefit of this teaching and believed and practiced it. It was the teaching of love for each other and oneness with the Great Source of Life. It was the same teaching that you people of Earth received centuries ago from the beloved One called Jesus the Christ. You loved your Teacher, but you misunderstood much of his teaching, and what you did understand you did not practice. Terrible cruelties were practiced by men on others who did not believe exactly as they did, on those whose ceremonies were different.

The great central teaching of love for God and mankind was neglected and importance was given to insignificant little differences in ritual.

Dear ones of Earth, many of you now have had your eyes – of the Spirit – opened and the true teaching of your beloved Master is understood and even practiced. Love – brotherly love – is coming forth into the world of humanity. In the midst of wars, chicanery, and greed, a spark of light is glowing.

It is called the New Age Teaching and it is the true teaching of Jesus the Christ, unadulterated and pure. Many groups on the Earth are studying and practicing this which is the truth.

We from the planet Uranus see this when we come close to the Earth. We watch and listen with love and rejoicing, and give our blessings and best wishes to the teachers and students of this true religion. Although the Earth is in turmoil, with battles and catastrophes, cruelty and misery, the little spark is growing, and is destined to spread over the whole Earth.

We of the planet Uranus will rejoice with you of Earth when this time comes.

It has been decided to give in this paper a very brief and simple explanation of astrology. In ancient times, astrology was a very deep study and was practiced by many who were prophets of coming events. The rulers of great and powerful nations had an astrologer always in their entourage and at their beck and call.

In modern times many private individuals have dabbled in astrology in a very superficial way, almost as a pastime, one might say. This writing will necessarily be brief but it will be accurate and true. Astrology is the study of the effect of the stars upon the planet Earth and its inhabitants. First of all we must admit that the stars do have an effect on the Earth and therefore all living beings on Earth feel the effect. But, as all good teachers explain, humanity does not have to be a slave to these effects.

When the signs of the zodiac are studied in connection with the birth date of an individual, that individual can take the predicted events as a possibility but not inevitable. He is endowed with freedom of choice and he may call on the God within him to guide him into a better path.

No man, woman or child is helpless because of what the stars show in his horoscope. The stars warn but cannot compel. What are the stars? They can be seen shining in the sky, especially when the atmosphere is clear and dry, as in the mountains or on the desert.

The sun is a star but it is not thought of in that way on Earth. It is the planets, shining with reflected light that are thought of and spoken of on Earth as stars.

That is the reason for this discourse. Uranus is one of the stars that influence the people of Earth. Venus, Jupiter, Saturn, Mercury are others. There is a magnetic current flowing from all of these bodies and it is felt by the living beings on each.

Every planet exerts a pull on others in its radius. The Earth affects those near it just as they affect the Earth. This was not understood by ancient astrologers but your modem astronomers know it. This pull is felt not only by the planet itself but by all that lives upon the planet. It can be of benefit or it can be detrimental to the living body.

Astrology was studied by wise men of old to foretell the futures of human beings, especially of kings and rulers. Usually, a king of a country had, among his courtiers, an astrologer who advised him according to what the stars showed in his horoscope. The day, month and year of birth of the ruler and the position of the planets at the time the horoscope was cast were studied by the astrologer, who drew up a chart and judged by that whether the time was propitious or not for entering into war or keeping the country in peace.

The prognostications were not always correct, and many an astrologer was executed by the command of an angry ruler, who had relied on his advice to enter into war only to be defeated.

At the present time, astrology is studied and practiced by private individuals who believe they can guide their daily actions by this knowledge.

It is a weak reed on which to lean, but in one way it can be used to advantage, and that is in the study of character. The stars that were in the sky at the time of birth do have an effect on the character and propensities of the subject. However, they do not compel the action of the one born under their rays. The man or woman whose strong desire is to lead a good life, by making an effort and having faith in prayer to God, can ignore the horoscope.

Some may say, "Then why bother with astrology at all?" This is a sensible question. The reason is that by knowing what the influences of the stars are in an individual's life, he is forewarned and will not allow himself to be guided by his emotions, but by careful consideration of the facts of a situation.

So now we shall briefly consider the effect of the various planets on the Planet Earth.

There are eight well known planets and from time to time the astronomers of Earth discover another which shows in their telescopes. These newer ones are not so close to the Earth and therefore have little effect on this planet.

The Planet Mars is near the Earth and the modem astronauts are eager to reach it and land upon it. It is not a large planet, but the vibrations from it have an effect on the Planet Earth.

For certain reasons the ancient astrologers were neglectful of this planet and confined their work to the larger planets in the solar system, of which the Earth is a part. Very important ones were Jupiter and Saturn.

They both have a very strong effect on the Planet Earth and therefore on the lives of the inhabitants of Earth. As shown in the horoscopes drawn up by the astrologers, Jupiter was a planet which brought happiness and good fortune, while Saturn had an opposite influence. The word "saturnine" in your language was derived from the name of the planet Saturn.

The rotation of the Earth and its movement around the sun bring it close to the other planets or far from them. So it comes under the influence of one planet or another depending on the position of the Earth itself. The Earth and the other planets, being spherical in shape, brings about a great variety of conjunctions, or close approaches of planets to each other.

The nearness of the planets is very important, for the strong vibrations that flow forth from each planet meet and mingle, bringing changes in the atmosphere and in the soil underfoot. The inhabitants of the planets feel this and it has an influence on their physical bodies, causing different emotions in the spiritual bodies.

So the study of astrology and also of astronomy is a study of the movements of the planets as they journey around the sun. In the study of astronomy, there is no attention paid to the effect this has on the human being. The study of astrology deals entirely with that phase.

In drawing up a horoscope, attention is paid to the exact location on Earth where the subject of the inquiry was born. This is very important, for the turning of the Earth will bring that spot into conjunction with a certain planet at a certain time. So the exact time of birth is also very important. All this has an effect upon the infant as it comes into the world and strongly influences the personality. In ancient times it was believed that this influence was too strong to be broken, but it has been found by the study of many subjects that this is not true, the spiritual being of man can triumph over any prognostication in a horoscope, and the spiritual being of man can reign supreme over any misfortune.

Man is spirit, not the body of flesh. The flesh body is the container only. The soul is spirit and lives forever; the physical body decays and is no more. It is very difficult for mankind to get the feeling of this. The physical body is so full of sensations, pains, aches, and thrills of joy. All actions in the outer world of living are seemingly performed by the physical body. From the time of birth, the little baby feels the sensations of the physical body, and so it continues until the end of physical life.

But the real being is the soul which lives the inner life, and the inner life is the life of spirit, not the life of matter. Spirit is everywhere; it is not confined to one locality. It cannot be held to one place; it goes out in thought everywhere.

This has been taught by the philosophers for ages, but man has largely ignored the teaching and has thought of himself as a physical body living the outer life. "As a man thinks in his heart, so is he."

Notice that the word "heart" is used in this well-known saying, not "mind." The heart is deep within; the mind is near the surface. The heart spoken of is not the physical organ; it is the spirit.

What has this to do with astrology? It has much to do with it, but it has largely been ignored. The effect of the planets on the physical being has been studied and recorded; the spirit has been entirely overlooked. The spirit is free and cannot be bound by rules and regulations, nor can it be a slave to the vibrations coming from the planets.

Herein is the power vested in humanity. As God is, so is humanity. God is all, all that is, including humanity. This is not blasphemy, it is truth. "In Him we live and move and have our being." The spirit – which is man – lives and moves in the One Spirit which is called God. This Great Spirit is everywhere. It is all. In It, by It and for It the human being lives, one with all Spirit, one with God, who is Spirit.

How can the physical effect of any planet near the Earth control the spirit of Man, which is one with the Spirit of God? It is only when the spirit of man allows the physical to take control that this can be. When this is understood, astrology can be a help to the individual. It will show what tendencies of character to guard against, and forewarn concerning events which may take place and could be guarded against.

It is not for recreation or to be carelessly dabbled in. If studied at all, it should be studied seriously. Too many persons merely play with it. Nothing that affects the spirit of man should be played with lightly, and astrology affects the spirit as well as the physical body. If one desires to make a real study of astrology, he can find a teacher without much difficulty; or, if he simply wishes to know how the stars affect his own life, he can find a genuine astrologer who will cast his horoscope for him, of course making a charge for the work.

The planet of which I am the Ruler, Uranus, is a large planet and its effect on the Earth and mankind is very strong. With her permission, I shall give as an example the experience of the one who is writing these words at my dictation.

Some years ago she was attending lectures given by a soul advanced in the new teaching. He again and again urged his hearers to give up the self and allow the Christ within to guide the life. She felt that she should do this, but hesitated because of fear that demands would be made on her that would be very difficult and unpleasant. She was thinking of this one day when the words came into her mind, "But think how much you will gain."

This gave her courage, and she decided to give herself up to God. So she prayed to God, saying, "Father, God, I give myself up to Thee, though I am only giving that which is Thine already." There was no answer, and she had not expected an answer, but a few days later she had the experience which was recounted at the beginning of this writing.

I, Uranus, poured my strong vibration into her and it was a shock at the time, but the effect that was left in her was joy and love. She has always been grateful for that experience.

Strong and sudden action is characteristic of Uranus. Strong and sudden, but never harmful, always beneficial, for it comes in love. The Planet Uranus, through me its leader, pours forth love and joy which flows through it from the Source of all creation, God.

God is all and all is God. There is no other anywhere. Life is all and all is Life. Life and God are synonymous words.

Now to go back to astrology. Astrology, seriously studied, can be an aid in living a good life. Astrology as a pastime can be dangerous. It is much better to give your heart and mind into the keeping of God, the Father of all, praying for His help and guidance. With these words, Uranus bids the people of Earth farewell.

**GOD OF SATURN**

## SATURN, PLANET OF PEACE, SENDS WARNING

This is the sixth paper from the planets in this solar system and it is from the Planet Saturn, spoken by the Ruler of that planet whose name is Saturn. It is coming to the people of Earth through the same human channel or instrument, as it is called. She has had much experience in receiving and writing from dictation from distant spheres. This is called telepathy. Now, after this introduction, we shall proceed with the writing of the sixth booklet.

There is a great desire among the planets near the Earth – and this is also felt by the Great White Brotherhood of the planes above the Earth – that mankind may learn to live in peace and love as the inhabitants of the other planets live.

It has been thought that if the inhabitants of the Earth were informed concerning the happy lives of the inhabitants of the other planets, it might inspire them to make an effort to achieve this peace and joy for themselves.

Now, after that rather lengthy introduction we shall confine ourselves to the planet Saturn. The people of Saturn are serious and much in earnest about everything they do, there is no foolishness or frivolity in their natures. This does not mean that they are gloomy or sad. No indeed, they are cheerful and happy, but not frivolous. They do not waste anything but make good use of everything they have.

They, like all the other planets except the planet Earth, live as the Great Teacher of Nazareth urged the people of Earth to live, in brotherly love. There is no greedy competition in business; there are no wars; there is no cheating; there is no selfishness of any kind. They live the life that the religious teachers, priests and ministers, preach and pray for.

It is the life of pure love, the only life of true joy and happiness. It is worth a kingdom to learn this and earn this. For it must be earned by most individuals, only a few come into the world perfect, without temptation. To strive after perfection is the first step and perseverance is the second. Never to criticize others but know that all have their temptations, and above all to know that within each one is the Spirit of Life or God, different names for the same Reality. This is the philosophy, or you may call it religion of the inhabitants of the planet Saturn. From early childhood we are instructed in this philosophy by our parents and they set us an example by living that which they teach.

The inhabitants of Saturn are not different looking than the prevailing race of the Earth, though there is a shining light in our eyes that is seldom seen in the eyes of mankind. It is the light of the God-presence shining out. You will see it in the eyes of some of the people of Earth but on Saturn it is in all without exception.

This is because we constantly feel the presence of God within us. This consciousness causes us to live together in perfect love and accord. Dear Ones of Earth, you can reach this same state of love and peace if you cultivate the constant feeling and belief in the presence of God within you.

I hear a question, has Saturn always been like that? Yes, we have always been like that and we daily give thanks for this knowledge. We have never asked for lives of free will, we have lived always according to the will of our Father God. Thus we have been saved from many mistakes and much unhappiness.

We firmly believe that the people of Earth are destined to attain this way of life and we urge you not to hesitate, but to give your-selves into the care and direction of your God.

Now, what about the daily lives of our people? How do we live? Have we a government and officials to manage the government? Have we laws and the enforcement of laws?

These questions shall be answered. Yes, we have a government and officials to manage it. All would be confusion without that. We have a government and officials and one supreme ruler. But here the likeness to your governments ceases. There is no necessity for law enforcement. Now this will seem very strange to you but it is true. Without any exception all those on this planet are law- abiding citizens. Certain rules and regulations have been decided upon in conference by the officials, and these rules are followed by every citizen without exception.

There is no poverty so there is no temptation to steal. The love of God is in every heart and this leads to love of each other. We are living the life that the Angels above the Earth sang of on Christmas Day.

You see we are well acquainted with your planet and its people. We hope that you will also become well acquainted with us and our planet. Without conceit we can say that a visit to Saturn would open your hearts and minds to much that you have never experienced on your Earth. It is our strong desire that you should visit us and see and experience for yourselves our way of living. We could come for you in our space ships, for they are real and solid. They are not ephemeral visions. We also have the hope that after you have visited us – of course your entire population could not come at one time – you would invite us – a group or committee to visit the Earth. Our best speakers could speak to gatherings of your people in various countries of your planet. We are able to speak all languages by intuition.

There are many fine groups in your country where they are studying and learning the truth of Life. We would be welcomed by these groups and the news of our coming would spread over all the country of America. This is not wishful thinking, it is a definite plan, and it is a plan not only for the Planet Saturn but for all the planets near the Earth. There are other planets in other solar systems in other universes, farther and farther out in space. There is no end to creation. It has always been and it shall always be, expanding and growing in immensity.

We all live in our own consciousness, which is not static bur constantly growing. Those who stop growing in understanding and expanding consciousness are unhappy and frustrated individuals. Those who are constantly seeking, yearning for more light, are happy individuals. This is the true nature that God gave to man on the Earth and to those who inhabit the other planets.

This does not mean that it is necessary to physically keep travelling about. Travelling physically to regions that are new to one is good. It wakens and stimulates the mind, but moving in the inner consciousness is a much greater experience. Constant expansion of consciousness is true living. "Seek and ye shall find, knock and it shall be opened unto you, ask and ye shall receive."

Yes, that is right, but do not settle down into inertia, continue seeking, knocking and asking. More and ever more understanding, greater and greater realization makes true living, joyous life. The law of life is growth. Look about you in the physical world and everywhere you will see growth.

You see plants growing from the seed; you see birds leaving the egg and growing from little naked creatures to flying singers of joyous songs. You see animals growing from helpless little creatures to activity in many forms, in forest and plane and as domesticated animals for use and for pleasure as pets. Growth is everywhere, but only the result of it is seen. The movement itself is not seen, it is invisible. God is not seen. He is invisible, but God is the living, acting cause of all that is seen, felt or experienced. God is all, there is no other.

You have grown from a baby to a grown man or woman by the action of God within you. Every little task that you perform is by the action of God. Of yourself you do nothing, God does all. It is difficult to understand and know that there is only God in existence. All is God and God is all.

We on Saturn know that – actually know it with our whole beings. Few people on the Earth have really learned that. They believe that they are separate from the Creator, living their own lives, performing their own actions. This the orthodox churches teach, just as they have for centuries, but the time has come when spiritual eyes are opening, spiritual minds and hearts are becoming active. The seed has been planted and growth is assured.

Man can look forward with assurance to a world of peace and love such as all the other planets are enjoying. But to have faith is not enough, action is required. The hearts of mankind must be opened to the action of God within. Feel the presence of God everywhere, in everything, and especially within the inner self, acting in response to your love and prayers.

This is the way we live on Saturn and it is our great desire that the people of Earth shall in the not too distant future be living thus also. If you would live like that for one day, you would make a decision to live like that forever.

We would like to visit your planet and speak in your synagogues and churches and in your advanced New Age groups. We hope that some time, not too far away, this may be accomplished. Meeting us and becoming friends with us, would make you realize that this that I am telling you is really true. You people of Earth would then feel a strong incentive to follow our example.

Your New Age groups have many large gatherings-conferences I believe they are called – where outstanding speakers are heard. We would like to be represented by one of our inspired speakers.

After listening to our speakers you may feel a stronger urge to visit our planet and spend some time travelling to our various cities, visiting our schools, our beautiful parks and recreation grounds. Also our government buildings must not be left out. You must attend a session of our legislature. I am sure you would find it interesting.

It meets in a large, handsome building in one of our cities. It is our only governing body and it makes the laws of the planet. The members of the legislative body are chosen by vote of the entire population of adults. There is no executive body, for this is not needed. All the population attends schools where these laws are studied and memorized. That is all that is needed. No one will knowingly break a law, so no police or jails are needed. All that is needed is for the people to know the laws. The law makers come together at regular intervals and review the laws. Sometimes they decide that a change should be made in one or more of them. If so, the law is written again with the change and given to the people to study.

A question may come to your mind. Are the people sometimes dissatisfied with a law? Yes, that sometimes happens, but not very often. The people come together and it is discussed. Next, a delegation is sent to discuss it with the legislative body. It is then decided whether to change it, keep it as it is, or eliminate it entirely.

The thought may have come to you that the cities must be very small or they could not let the whole population discuss these matters. You are right; the cities are more the size of what you call villages. The difference is not in the size but in the appearance. The buildings are large and handsome, built of the finest and most enduring materials. The schools, shops, every kind of building, are of strong, beautiful material. The only way in which villages are resembled is in the size of the population.

This small population is a great advantage, as is easily seen. The planet Saturn is a true democracy, a government of the people by the people. The planet is large, but it is divided into many small parts called cities. Each one of these is self governing. The laws are not made for the planet as a whole, any more than the laws of your country are made for the planet Earth as a whole. Remember that Saturn is a large planet. The large legislative body that I spoke of could be thought of as a body resembling the League of Nations. However, this is not a very good comparison, for the League of Nations represents separate and widely different nations, while the central legislative body on Saturn represents similar cities with populations of one blood.

Your cities in your United States each have a mayor, elected by the people, and a city council. They look after small affairs immediately concerning the city. Above the city government is the state government at the head of which is the Governor. Beyond this is the national government at the head of which is the President.

Our legislative government is very similar to this. It is our administrative government that is different. As I said before, we do not need law enforcement bodies. We do not need lawyers to argue cases or judges to decide the case. The population of each small city, or village as you might call it, has studied and learned the laws and nobody ever goes contrary to any law.

Our people live in an atmosphere of love and unselfishness. It begins in the homes and spreads out from there into all regions of the planet. How happy we would be if your Earth had an atmosphere like this.

It is not that you do not know right from wrong, but greed has taken possession of you. Greed – what a hideous thing is greed! It is seen in all parts of the Planet Earth, in all nations. Nation fights nation, race fights race, and if you look for the cause it is always greed. The stronger despoils the weaker and all over the planet there is fear and struggle. It is like the animals of the forest, where the stronger kill and devour the weaker.

When we travel over the planet Earth we see this everywhere, and our hearts ache at the sight. Almost everywhere there are churches and teachers, but sermons are listened to on Sunday and forgotten the rest of the week. It is not because of ignorance that man lives like this. If it were it could be changed by teaching. No, there is a darkness over the Earth like a pall. In this darkness there are beings of sinister purpose. It is not as if there were one Satan trying to destroy the people, no, not one but many. These are the dark spirits of greed. They have been called by different names, but by any name they are fiends. They are like vampire bats sucking the blood of the people. Some have passed out of the physical body but they are just as dangerous-maybe more dangerous-than the ones in physical bodies.

We have hesitated to speak about this for it seemed too horrible to mention. However some of your truly great Teachers are speaking and the situation is becoming known. Some call them watchers, and some call them money-changers, but these are the same. As I have said, they are vampire bats sucking the blood of the people.

Your governing bodies do not belong to these groups. Thank God for that. We of the planet Saturn have felt forced to speak of what we see as we come close to the Earth. It is painful to do so, for this will be a great shock to the innocent hearts and minds of many.

It is known by some few groups, and the news is being spread by writing and speaking. What are these dark ones, you ask. The answer is to be found in the Apocrypha of the Bible. The Apocrypha is a part of the Bible that has been separated from the rest, being considered untrue or spurious.

It tells about the fallen angels which were driven out of heaven and, led by Lucifer, their leader, have tempted and influenced mankind to break the commandments of God. They especially encourage greed and unbrotherly actions of all kinds; but greed predominates. With the greed is pride and conceit. Many of them are in high positions in money making organizations. These organizations are manipulated so as to make exorbitant profits for the share holders, who come from the ranks of these schemers. They came upon the Earth centuries ago and have remained, practicing their nefarious trade.

They carry on their activities in secret. On the surface they appear to be ordinary business men – very prosperous ones. We of Saturn can see them and read their minds. They are of a different breed, you might call it, from the rest of humanity, but they appear to be simply portly, ostentatious, successful business men.

In their secret meetings they show their real colors. We of the planets near the Earth can see them from our ships and also when we travel in our bodies near the Earth. We do not stay long for the atmosphere is extremely disagreeable. This atmosphere is all around the planet Earth, but the worst of it is beyond the sight of the people of Earth. The worst smog of your big cities is nothing compared to this.

These creatures and their actions have now been discovered by some of the people of the Earth and they are doing their best to make known that which they have discovered. They call themselves "The Sons of Jared," for Jared was the name of one in ancient times who exposed these demons and fought against them.

We of the other planets have decided that we should come out in the open and make this known. We would not be good friends of our brothers on Earth if we kept silent when we can see clearly what is going on. Many people have not been able to believe what has been told by the "Sons of Jared," it has seemed too fantastic and improbable. I assure you it is true, though it seems too horrible to be true. All the people of the Earth should rise up and fight against it. Not with bombs and firearms, but with 40 words. It is now known only in the United States of America and in only a small group there.

If you study the book of Revelation in your Bible you will find these creatures spoken of there. We, of all the other planets, urge the people of Earth to do something to stop this horror. It is not the planet Saturn alone telling you about this. Saturn is the spokesman for all the planets.

There is something that I should make clear to you. The darkness around the Earth does not come direct from these Watchers or Money Changers. No, it is from the dark forces that are attracted by them.

These dark forces are followers of Lucifer, who was once the prince of Light, but who tried to usurp the power of God Almighty and was expelled from heaven. He came to Earth with his followers and has ever since been tempting mankind in every way possible. Some human beings have not required much temptation to make them greedy and selfish; others have fought against it; others have never felt the temptation, for they loved their God with all their heart and their fellow men as themselves.

These forces of darkness know where they will be received. Some are in human form and enter into the outer events of society and into business affairs, others are invisible to the human eye. They sometimes take possession of the inner life of a man or woman.

In the New Testament of your Bible it tells how Jesus drove the evil spirits from within those who had fallen prey to them. These evil spirits, or others similar to them, are active now, in this so-called civilized age. They can be cast out now as they were in olden times, by prayer to the Father, Son and Holy Ghost.

It was said by the Master Jesus that constant vigilance was necessary, for when the evil spirit was driven out and the house was swept and garnished, it would find seven more worse than itself and enter in again, and the last state of that man would be worse than the first.

This is all literally true. It is not just a symbolic story, it is actual fact. Oh, people of Earth, wake up and look about you and when you look about do not fail to also look within, for you, unaware, may be harboring one of these evil spirits. They manifest as selfishness, greed, cruelty. They have no love for others, all their thought is centered in themselves. They are imps of Lucifer, who is on the Earth seeking whom he may destroy.

Do not be too sure that you are safe. Call on God and the Great White Brotherhood for protection. The members of the Great White Brotherhood are servants of God and instructors and guides of humanity.

You may wonder how we of another planet can know so much that you on the Earth are ignorant of. You know that often a strange visitor to a house may understand the family better than they do themselves. A certain detachment seems necessary for perfect understanding. Eyes may become dim from constantly looking on the same thing. A new scene is more easily discerned. When the true situation is seen and understood, then means of combating it may be instituted. Discussion groups should come together everywhere in all nations of the Earth.

In the near future there will come a time when the United States of America will fall under the influence of dark forces. Their leaders will conspire with hostile countries in order to win elections over the true winners. Once they gain power, they will make it difficult for anyone to hold office except those who have aligned themselves with the forces of evil. During these times, Lucifer and his forces will pollute the minds of the citizens of the United States with prejudice against other races, religions and even those of different sexual orientation. These are the same evil beings that helped create Nazi Germany, fascism, and Communism at its very worst.

Before the dark time, the United States will be coming out of a great economic downturn; however, it will also mark a time of great social progress, equality and spiritual growth among the peoples of the nation. Its President will be a great man who is intelligent, wise and beloved by many. However, the next President will be aligned with evil and darkness. Many religious leaders will join him, believing that God has chosen this President to be the savior of the nation. But they too, because of their personal prejudices and hatred of people they view as "different," have succumbed to the hideous darkness.

This Presidents intention is to create chaos and uncertainty. In fact, he thrives and feeds off of creating and inciting upheaval. He will attack without pity and no one will be safe from his hatred. He will forge a cult of followers who will embrace his lies and be willing to throw away all moral sensibilities and humanity at his command. Other nations will tremble in fear of this President, knowing that evil has engulfed him and the United States.

During these dark days, we will work harder than we have ever worked before. Humanity is at the threshold of living or dying because of what will happen in the United States. There will be groups dedicated to righteousness and good who will work to battle the pestilence of evil that will overrun the country. There will be groups in all the states. The people of the nation will be aroused and their minds will grasp the situation, and energy will be called forth to drive away the evil forces of darkness. This can be done by pouring forth the Light. Call for the Light of God which never fails to destroy the darkness.

Send forth love to the bewildered ones who are terrified and feel helpless. There is much for the illumined ones of Earth to do. The Great Brotherhood has always been helping mankind by instruction and leadership. Now they are planning to branch out into many other sections of the country, for they know that the situation is precarious all over the nation, and in fact all over the planet Earth. If the United States of America is saved much help can be given to the other countries of the Earth.

You who are reading this can help. Pray more than once or twice a day. Send forth love to all mankind. Know that God will answer your call for it has been said, "Ask and you shall receive."

This admonition has not been heeded as it should be. It should not be an occasional asking, but daily, hourly the mind and heart should rise to the Source of all good and the call for help should go up. It need not be a long, involved prayer, a few words are all that are needed, and the force of it is in the faith and love that are in the petition.

Every man, woman and child could do this. If they do, the Earth will be protected from the machinations of Lucifer and the dark forces. They cannot operate in an atmosphere of love. Wars and riots, greed and selfishness are their sustenance and strength.

Deprive them of this and fill the atmosphere with love, faith in God and humanity, and the evil beings will flee away, for they will find nothing to feed on.

Do not wait, time is precious and the sooner you start to work the better. This can be done by individuals all over the Earth. It is not necessary to form groups but groups are effective for man is gregarious, and working together brings confidence, and confidence assures results.

At the present time there are large groups in California, Vermont, New Mexico, New York, New Zealand and in other countries. They are all sending out much light, but the help of private individuals in their own homes is greatly needed. A great sheet of light should shine all over the planet Earth so that no darkness can obscure it and no evil spirit can get through it. They are terrified and flee when the light is turned upon them.

This is the warning of the Planet Saturn, and all the other planets join with all their hearts.

With love and blessings to the Planet Earth from all her sister planets, the Planet Saturn now says farewell.

The inhabitants of Saturn are not different looking than those of the Earth, though there is a shining light in our eyes that is seldom seen in the eyes of mankind. It is the light of the God-presence shining out.

**GOD OF JUPITER**

## FROM JUPITER, THE PLANET OF JOY

The speaker is the Ruler of a large planet to which man has given the name Jupiter. Jupiter is the name by which the ancient Romans designated the Ruler of all the Gods. The Greek name was Zeus, but it was the same God. English speaking people were more familiar with Rome than with Greece, so they used the Roman name for this planet.

Now that I have introduced myself I shall proceed to give my message. The history of this planet is not all heaven nor is it all hell. We have never fallen into the depths nor have we risen, as a people, into the celestial heights of perfection. However, I would say that there is more of heaven than of hell in our lives.

We are of one race, which makes understanding much easier than if there were many races, as there are on the Earth. We are not a very tall people as they are on Venus, but neither are we very short; I suppose we are what you would call a medium height. Also our complexion and the color of our hair is medium, it is what you call brunette. So much for our appearance.

Now for the planet on which we live. The climate varies just as the Earth's does, and for the same reason; we are not stationary, we move around the sun and we also rotate as we move. We have summer and winter, day and night, but because of the large size of the planet, the seasons are longer, as are the periods for day and night.

Our bodies are of flesh, blood, bone and muscle as yours are, and we also have a system of nerves like yours. So we feel comfortable or uncomfortable depending on the warmth or coolness of the weather, just as you do. So, indeed we are brothers and sisters of yours, and we wish to tell you so. We extend to you an invitation to visit our planet and be our guests in our homes. We could take you on a tour of the whole planet, visiting our cities and our beautiful pleasure resorts in the open country.

You would find no extreme poverty here and no extreme wealth, for we have always been guided by moderation and a strong feeling of brotherhood. It is natural to us to be kind and generous, just as it is in a large number of your population, the difference is that with us it is all; none are greedy or cruel.

You may be wondering how I can know so much about your planet Earth. Of course you know that we can come close to the Earth in our ships of the air, but you probably do not know that without a ship we can come close to your planet, near enough to see and watch you moving about on the land and sea. Our bodies can be made light at will, so that we can travel through the air just as easily as on the land.

Our planet is one of those whose population is able to do this. I have been told that many of you Earth people, in your sleep at night, dream of flying through the air in the human body alone. This is because eons ago the people of Earth could do that, as we can now.

We all pray that the time may soon come when you, our brothers, may do that again. It is a joyous feeling to rise into the air and fly like a bird, but without the need for wings. Those that you call Angels do that. They have no wings and have no need for them. Pure joy and radiant light is all that is needed to make the body rise above the drawing power of the Earth.

It is easy and natural for you to walk upon the surface of the earth now, but when the Golden Age has arrived, once more you will be able to fly above the Earth, high in the air. There are also other forgotten abilities that shall be yours. One is the ability to precipitate solid matter from the air about you. Your saints and prophets did this centuries ago, and long before that the entire population was able to do so.

When the saints and prophets performed these acts it was considered miraculous, but thousands of years before it was as simple and natural as eating or drinking. We on Jupiter still find it so, and we would be very happy to instruct our brothers and sisters of Earth in this, to us, simple art. Food, drink and clothing can be created this way, so no one need be hungry or cold.

You, dear ones of Earth, have lost the ability to do these things because ages ago you forgot the Source of all life, from which all creation flows forth. Some of your churches still sing a beautiful little hymn, "Praise God from whom all blessings flow, praise Him all creatures here below, praise Him above Ye heavenly host, praise Father, Son and Holy Ghost."

This is sung, but the words do not have their true meaning deep in the heart. It has been forgotten and no longer is known, or rather felt instinctively, that God only performs all actions. The word God, as used here, means the Great Power which is the Source of all that is, was, or ever shall be. Mankind forgot and wandered away from the Source of All Being, giving himself, the little human self, all the credit for his accomplishments.

The little human self has never had the ability to perform any act, even the simplest. Not even an arm can be raised without the power of God within. This is done without doubt, and is learned in innocent babyhood. It is true that the baby does not think as an adult thinks, and in this fact is the joy and beauty of the infant's life. He moves his arms and legs by instinct and there is no doubt felt. Every motion that he makes is developing the muscles of his little body. These movements are joy to him, and pure joy is health. He feels the love of his parents and love for them is born in him.

Like this was man in the beginning. He lived by instinct, as the birds and animals do. Joy was in his being-the joy of life. He did not doubt, but lived life as it came to him. When he began to think, he also began to doubt. Why were thinking and doubting connected? Because he had lost the deep feeling of oneness with the source of all life and was living on the surface. In his thinking he was mistaken, he believed that each human being was a separate entity, living his own life by his own power.

Before he began to think he felt, deep within his being, the truth of life, and knew, without trying to reason, that there was a greater power than his own little self, acting within and through him. He did not try to reason, he simply felt that this was so.

At the present time on Earth, another change has come to vast numbers of people; they both think that which is true, and feel it in the depths of their being. Now man feels his oneness with God, the Creator, and also understands in his mind.

We of Jupiter rejoice with mankind, for we for many eons have understood, and practiced that which we understood and felt. Life should be pure joy, and is when it is understood and accepted as it is. What is it? It is love, pure divine love. Centuries ago this was taught on the planet Earth, but it was accepted in the lives and living of a comparatively small number, the others believed in force and force is still, at this present time, being practiced all over the Earth.

Dear brothers of Earth, open your hearts and your eyes and join the other planets in living lives of peace, not conflict.

This writing was not intended to be a sermon, but perhaps it seems to be one. I hope it will not be misunderstood. We of the planet Jupiter extend to you a most cordial invitation to visit us, and we will be most happy to come to the Earth in our ships of the air, and carry you to our planet for a visit to all the places of interest and beauty. Above all we would like you to meet us in our homes, and have friendly chats with us.

Speaking for all the inhabitants of the Planet Jupiter, I, Jupiter give you of Earth our sincere love and friendship.

**The Jupiter Command is the overseer of the cosmic gateway to the solar system. This allows fleets of lightships from all points of the galaxy to enter nearby space.**

**MONKA OF THE TRIBUNAL COUNCILS**

**GODDESS OF VENUS**

## INVITATION FROM THE PLANET VENUS

**T**his is coming to you from Venus and is dictated by the Ruler of Venus, who also is named Venus, the Goddess of Love. I have always been the ruler of this planet and always shall be, for such is the law. One ruler who is satisfactory to the people, and who lives forever.

Many of you may not believe this, for on the planet Earth every human body dies, though the spirit in that body lives forever in a higher plane of consciousness. The human body becomes old and worn out, or becomes sick and destroyed by disease. This does not take place on Venus.

The planet Venus is our home now and shall be forever. We are happy in our lives, living in love and perfect unselfishness. Everything on our planet might be called perfect. At the present time this cannot be said of the planet Earth. It is a common saying, "nothing is perfect." Some earnest ones are called perfectionists, for they always aim at perfection, and sometimes do attain it. There are inventions which are acting perfectly, but most of them could be improved.

One of these inventions is your airplane. It is wonderful that man, after the struggle of centuries, has produced a ship of the air that flies easily and very rapidly the greatest distances on the planet. The fuel gasoline is used and it is used in your automobiles also. A machine using this fuel moves as rapidly and as far in distance as anyone could desire, but there is one flaw which is very serious. Very noxious fumes pour from the vehicles.

These fumes are injurious to the health of the inhabitants of the Earth, human, animal and vegetable. There is a way to prevent these fumes, and that is, do not use gasoline.

We who live on other planets near the planet Earth get our fuel from the atmosphere. Your scientists could learn this from the other planets if you would become friends and accept our offer. I briefly touch on this and we now return to the planet Venus.

Those of you who have studied the mythology of Greece and Rome know that the names of the planets were taken from the names of Gods and Goddesses of the Greek and Roman religion. In your Earth thinking and belief in this century, this religion is only myth or fairy tale, and you may be shocked when I say that it is truth.

I am the Venus who was called the Goddess of love and beauty, but there is a difference in the meaning of these terms "love and beauty." They, on the Earth, have lost their true meaning of pure, spiritual Love and pure, spiritual Beauty, and are used with the meaning of physical beauty and sensuous love.

As I have already told you, the people of Venus are very happy and contented. All put others before themselves, give with joy and receive with gratitude. It is an ideal life and there is no reason that it may not last forever.

Now it is our greatest desire to help the inhabitants of the Earth to understand and know the possibility of living such a life. With us it is not a beautiful dream of the distant future, it is a present fact. This can become a fact on the planet Earth, but education must come first.

Man must be taught, as children are taught in school. It is necessary to learn first what can be, by knowing what already is on the neighboring planets.

It is not an impossibility for the Earth people to live perfect lives of joy and perfection, but it will require first of all a sincere desire to attain this perfection. Before desire there must be belief that this can be, and that it already is in other places. This we are trying to show you by giving ourselves as examples.

The base of our civilization rests on a strong love and worship of the One Great Source of all life, the One God above all Gods, the Creator and Sustainer of all life. God is Life, God is Love, God is Light. God is everywhere, in everything, from the tiniest blade of grass to the Universe of Universes.

Many of you Earth people know this and rejoice in the knowledge, but there are more who do not know it. They believe in a God outside of creation, in a heaven far away in the sky, a severe God who punishes His children for their sins and mistakes.

A God such as this never existed. We of Venus have always known the truth and loved with all our hearts the God of Love, in whom is all life, love and power. With-out Him nothing would be, for all is in Him and He is in all.

It is very difficult if not impossible to express the truth, for God is not a being that can be called He, nor can this being be called she. Recently the words Father-Mother have been used in an effort to ex-press the truth, but they fail to express it.

The great Source of all life is formless. Being everywhere, how could it have a form? It is in every living thing, in insects, birds, beasts, human beings, plants and even stones; it is in the air, water, soil.

It is consciousness everywhere and we live in that consciousness. We are all formed in that consciousness, live and have our being in it. It is All. There is nothing else anywhere, in anything. It is impossible to express this, although It is expression, everywhere expressing everything.

It expresses in forms, your forms, our forms, all forms. The cause of the forms is formless. No words can express the truth of life, but the human heart can love and adore that which the human mind is unable to express. The truth can be felt even though it cannot be expressed. This is so everywhere, in all the planets, in all the universes, in the great everywhere without beginning, without end, which it is impossible for any mind to grasp.

But though our minds cannot grasp this truth our hearts can and do love it. It is our great desire that not only a few of Earth's people, as now, know this truth, but that every individual on the planet Earth may know and rejoice in it.

When this is so there will be peace in-stead of war, plenty instead of poverty. There will be love instead of harsh criticism and dislike. As the wise of the Earth have already told you "peace must begin with me" – with each one. From there it will flow out to all mankind. Not only to all mankind, but to animals also. No longer will there be shooting of deer and birds for pleasure – sport it is called. The American Indians were above doing this; they killed by necessity, for they had not learned to raise enough grain on which to sustain life. It was necessary for them to eat meat, but they never killed for sport.

The machine age has played a good part in freeing horses and oxen from the drudgery of hard work under the whips of their owners. How we of Venus rejoiced when we saw this take place.

I feel a thrill of surprise in the one who is writing this, and from this judge that those who read may also be startled to know that we can look at the planet Earth and see quite clearly what is going on in the fields and or the streets.

We also have instruments, and very good ones. You call your instruments for long distance seeing, telescopes. We have a different name in our language but it means the same. These instruments are very efficient and we can look onto the planet Earth and see much of that which is going on.

We do not intrude on your privacy by looking into your houses, but that which is in the open we can see. We shall be willing and pleased when you can see what we are doing in our fields and streets. You will then no longer be afraid of us. You will see that we are beings like yourselves. We have our shops, business offices and places of entertainment. We love music and art of all kinds. We play games of skill and dexterity but never games that become battles as some of yours do.

We are your friends, as the inhabitants of all the planets are, and our great desire is that you may visit us and see for yourselves how we live and what kind of beings we are. Only close contact can give you a true knowledge of our lives. This writing can give you information. It can dispel wrong beliefs and replace them with the truth, but only meeting us and knowing us can give you realization of what we truly are.

To realize you must enter into our actual everyday lives, meet our little children as well as our statesmen and business men. You must see our beautiful flowers and trees, our lakes and streams, our sunshine, and showers.

We invite you to come and experience all this with us. Some few of you have actually been taken into a space ship and brought here, but most of these have not been in the physical body. They have travelled in the etheric body, leaving the physical on the Earth. This is good but not quite the same as coming in your physical bodies, for we are in physical bodies, living and carrying on all our affairs in physical bodies. So you can understand that in order to have a perfectly natural contact you should come to us in physical bodies.

You can do that if you are willing to board one of our ships of the air, and trust us to bring you to our planet. Then, after your visit, we would return you to the Earth. This would be done with each planet. But, as I explained before, if you learn to build your own spacecraft you could travel from planet to planet in perfect freedom.

We shall now continue on our imaginary visit to the planet Venus. Our lives are not entirely different from yours. In fact, they are quite similar to yours in many respects. The one great difference is that we live entirely in love – pure, divine love. There are no quarrels, no destructive criticism; all is peace and true love. I was about to say brotherly love, but on the Earth, brothers, even though they may love each other, often have relapses, when they quarrel and have very bitter, unbrotherly feelings. On Venus this is never so. Even the tiny tots never quarrel.

This is the great difference between our planets. To the outer vision there is not so much difference in what you shall see. We have cities, farms, mountains, plains, all quite similar to yours at a casual glance, but on investigation a great difference is found.

We have no slums, no poverty anywhere. Also there is no extreme wealth. All the people are living in comfort and in pleasant surroundings. The cities are not devoid of trees and flowers. Our large cities are not crowded, but are spread over enough territory to comfortably accommodate the population. There are many play grounds for the children, so they do not have to play on the streets and sidewalks.

But there is something that is better than these outer things, and that is a serene inner joy that is felt by every living being. This peace and love that is felt by every person goes forth into the atmosphere and is felt by animals and birds. The peace of God which is in the center of every living thing.

Spiritual ones on the earth feel it, not always perhaps, but at times. It is a peace that prevails over all emotions of worry, doubt or fear. It is serene and joyful. Divine love for all creation brings the peace of God which is triumphant over all emotions. When you enter our large cities, this is felt as strong as in the open country, or in the forests or mountains. This is not so on the Earth. There men seek the great open spaces to find peace and rest. Those of you who have gone into these quiet places on your planet will know of what I mean on the Earth because of reports in the newspapers concerning the discussions and theories of scientists. Some very powerful instruments are now in use which have given more information than has ever been had before concerning the planet Mercury.

We shall not discuss the theories and speculations of the scientists. Our effort shall be devoted to persuading mankind to accept the friendship of the inhabitants of the planets in the solar system in which the Earth rotates. We know that we are living beings just as you know that you are living beings. There is no theory or speculation about it. It is the truth.

All the planets will send more space ships of various kinds onto the Earth in order to attract the attention of more and more people. We are very well informed concerning the geography of the Earth, and we know where the open spaces suitable for landing are located.

There is little more to be said in this writing. One thing more, we have not yet described our personal looks. What do we look like? We have faces and bodies like yours but there are differences, which I will mention. We are a very tall people and all of us are golden blonds with blue eyes. We have not the variety that you have of blond, brunette or red-head, nor are there great differences in height as there is on Earth. No one is much under six feet and many are well over that.

You may think that this would be monotonous but we are used to it and do not notice any monotony, for each is an individual mentally and spiritually, even though we have hair of the same color.

To us who live on Venus the inner expression of individuals is very much more important than the outer form of body, face or hair.

I, Venus, speaking for the people of Venus, now say farewell to the Earth and another will take my place. We send you our love and our blessings.

**Venusians have been traveling to Earth in their spaceships for thousands of years**

**A Space Brother from the planet Venus as
imagined by Gene Duplantier**

**GOD OF MERCURY**

## PLANET MERCURY SENDS GREETINGS

This is the second in a series of writings concerning the space ships of the planets in the solar system of which the Earth is part. I shall give you my name and the name of the planet that I rule. It is one and the same, Mercury. It is not a strange name to mankind, for centuries- ago it was known to man as the name of One who was called the messenger of the Gods. He wore a cap, on each side of which were wings, and on his feet were wings, while in his hand he carried a staff around which a serpent was wound.

He moved very swiftly through the air, carrying messages from one God to another in the solar system. The Earth people of that day knew nothing of solar systems. They thought that the Earth was flat and the stars, moon, and sun moved above it; but they did have some information concerning the Gods and Goddesses above the earth, although much of their belief was erroneous.

At the present time on Earth, man is also mistaken concerning the other planets about the Earth. To him they have been uninhabited, and the stories told about the Gods and Goddesses have been only fables, charming and beautiful subjects for the pictures of great artists, or for statues and beautiful poems. They were not believed to be fact – real, living beings.

I can assure you that they are real, living Beings, and always have been such. The Earth is only a small planet in a system of planets which is called the solar system. It is one solar system among many in the Universe and the Universe is one Universe among many Universes. I, who speak to you, am the God or Ruler of the Planet Mercury, which has my name. It is a small planet very close to the earth. You may be disappointed to know that I do not have wings on my cap or on my heels, nor do I carry the caduceus. I do not need these to fly with. I can fly through space without the assistance of any wings or mechanical aid. I do, however, at times use a spacecraft in order to have with me others from my planet. It is the same as people on Earth traveling together.

The spacecraft that we use are not all alike; there are a number of shapes and sizes. The first that modern men saw with the sun shining on them, looked round and concave, so they called them flying saucers. They were not exactly the shape they appeared to be as they moved swiftly over the Earth. Later, others were seen which were long and "cigar shaped." These long ones were seen to land on the Earth and discharge smaller ships of a different shape. Some were round and some the shape of a mushroom.

It has been said – and truly – that hundreds of space ships flew over Washington, D.C. at one time. Many people saw them, but the government has always suppressed the news of the appearance of these craft. More and more individuals have been seeing them, usually over open space, plains, and flat prairies, though occasionally over the mountains, or even over, and close to, a city street. The visits of these craft are no secret, try though the government may to make it so.

There is also a plan which no inhabitant of Earth can stop-and it is for the benefit of the inhabitants of Earth-and that is for a series of writings such as this. One little book from each planet. This is the second one, and one by one the others shall follow. This one shall deal with Mercury.

Our planet is small, but it is throbbing with life and activity. The climate is mild and beautiful. The air is pure and clean for there are no poisonous sprays used, there are no fumes given off from our vehicles, in which the people travel from place to place on the planet, or from the great space ships which carry us from planet to planet.

This can no longer be said of our sister planet, the Earth. Not so very long ago the air of the Earth was as pure as ours, but alas, it is now dense with fumes which are called smog. But the readers of this book know too well that this is so. We shall now turn our attention entirely to the planet Mercury.

The government might be called paternal, for one ruler is always at the head of it, but you might call it fraternal for the people discuss and decide many things - in fact almost all of the laws that govern the planet, for laws are necessary in any civilization. There is only one race on the planet and all is one nation. I must admit that this makes government much simpler than it is on Earth.

The weather is not the same evenly all over the surface of the planet. Heat and cold vary from one location to another. Most of the planet has what you would call a moderate climate, while some parts are warmer, and others cooler.

Farming is carried on with success in most locations, and even the cities have gardens of beautiful flowers, and the streets are all lined with trees. This can be found in many places on your Earth even now, but the cities are becoming bleaker as the population increases and in many of them trees and flowers are not found.

I feel sure you would enjoy a visit to Mercury, and you would be welcomed most cordially and taken on tours of the planet. We have many very fine hotels, where you would find comfortable and beautiful rooms for the guests, and most delicious food. Those who greeted you would be your hosts, and your tour of the planet would cost you nothing. You would be sure to have a happy time, and would see nothing to rouse your sympathy and make you unhappy, as is the case when touring certain parts of the Earth.

There is no poverty on Mercury and no excessive wealth. There are no classes of highly educated and ignorant. All are educated and intelligent. This may be almost beyond your imagination, but it is the truth. I shall tell you what is the cause of this idyllic life.

It is what the angels sang to the Earth on the day that Christ was born, "Glory to God in the highest and on Earth peace, goodwill toward men." We on Mercury live this in our daily lives. Our hearts sing always, "Glory to God and love to our fellows." We feel that all of us are brothers and all are equal. All have equal rights, there is no privileged class or underprivileged class. No one is hungry for anything, either physical or spiritual.

We of Mercury are looking forward expectantly to the time when the scientists of Earth shall have accepted our help in constructing a spaceship such as ours. Then the people of Earth can come to us as we now go to them. They can fly easily and quietly from planet to planet visiting, and accepting our brotherly hospitality. For we feel that we are your brothers and sisters – we know that we are.

It makes our hearts ache to see the cruelty and greed of the Earth people and their destructive treatment of the planet, which was so beautiful. Our hearts never ache for anyone on our planet, for all is peace and happiness.

We can hear you asking, "Has this always been the condition on Mercury?" The answer is, "No, we passed through a very unhappy period, very similar to that which the Earth is going through at the present time. Some individuals who were in business – for there were businesses of various kinds – looked about at their fellows and thought of ways to take advantage of them, thus accumulating more money with which to buy luxuries for themselves at the expense of their trusting clients."

This was the beginning of a situation such as you have on Earth at present. We forgot God, from whom all blessings flow, and thought only of ourselves. Some were grasping, so others retaliated, and thus began a long period of time in which we lived as you on Earth are living now. Some of the people lived in great luxury, while others had not enough food to nourish their bodies, and not enough good clothing to keep them warm. This condition became worse, until I, who was the supreme Ruler of the planet, and the ones who had advisory positions in the government, realized that something must be done to stop and change this deplorable situation.

So we met together and went into the stillness of deep meditation, opening our hearts and minds to receive the instruction which came to us from the Life within us, which flowed from the Source of all that Is. Then we saw clearly where the trouble lay.

We called on all the leaders in every town and hamlet to do as we had done; get together in deep meditation and let the Life, or God, within them give them the answer, for when they in this way understood, and could see what was the cause of the trouble, they then would receive inspiration from the Voice within them directing them in the proper procedure. It was necessary to warn the people of the danger which threatened the whole planet because of the greed and selfishness of a few individuals, which was spreading like a disease and drawing more and more active business into these nefarious practices.

Fortunately for our planet there were no large cities but many small towns. The governing officials of each town called a meeting, explained the situation, and warned the people of the danger to the population as a whole because of the greed of a few.

They lifted their hearts in prayer to the Great Source of all Being, which was the Life within each one of them. They prayed for guidance, and it was received and followed. Many illumined Souls on Earth have individually practiced this in their own lives, meditating daily, or oftener, several times a day, raising their consciousness into the spiritual realm and receiving the answer, which changed perplexity into certainty, and a clear course of procedure was followed. This which has been done, and is being done by individuals in their private lives, can be also followed in the government of cities and countries.

The officials of the government could follow this plan, and the individual citizens could call for the blessing and help of the Great Source of all Life, to open the hearts and minds of both leaders and followers, so that wisdom would be the guide. Wisdom and love always go hand in hand.

You who are reading this can practice this in your own lives, for yourselves and for your government. Send forth love over all the Earth, bless all the nations, beginning with your own private life, then your country, and finally all the Earth.

This is the way the planet Mercury was saved from the extremes of poverty and wealth, from greed and brutality, and war. We can advise you people of the Planet Earth because we have saved ourselves from a like condition. We are grateful, when we look into the Planet Earth and see the misery and crime there, that we are able to give the nations and the individuals the true story of our own experience. What we have done you can do. It may be more difficult, because the remedy has not been applied as soon as we did, but it can be done.

At the present time we see a tremendous uplift among the inhabitants of Earth. Light is shining in the darkness and is spreading fast from the United States of America, where freedom was the aim of the Founding Fathers of the country. Their example has not been followed by those who came after them and there is much poverty and crime in the country but the spark that they lit has never died, and now it is growing in size and brightness.

In the midst of the turmoil and the horrors in the world of the Earth, a great power for good is increasing, fed by the love and devotion of thousands-no, millions of dedicated ones. They are those who have been receiving the New Age Teaching, and who are practicing that which they have learned and believe with all their hearts.

Saint Germain was the instigator of this movement, which is spreading over the Earth, but Jesus the Christ, who came onto the Earth centuries ago and gave his life for mankind, was the savior of mankind, at a period of time when it seemed that mankind and the Earth itself must perish.

There are many forms of this teaching, many leaders and many groups. It may seem strange that One from another planet should tell you this, but sometimes a stranger sees more clearly, and without any of the prejudice that has handicapped those living in the midst of a situation.

All these active groups are guided by Teachers from the Great White Brotherhood, though some of them do not know this. They have fanned the spark of brotherly love that still smoldered on the Earth, and we can now see the light brightening and spreading in many parts of the Earth, but especially in the United States of America.

In earlier days the oppressed citizens of other countries fled to America in search of freedom, and there they settled and made it their home. But, alas, those who had fled from persecution began to persecute others of different religions, who had followed them. At that time there were only separate colonies on the Western continent, all settled by people who had come in search of freedom to worship God according to their beliefs.

But the beliefs of the people who sought freedom differed in minor ways and, as it had been in Europe, it now was in America, the stronger persecuted the weaker and there was no freedom that was universal.

There still is no true freedom anywhere on the Planet Earth. But the love of freedom and the desire for it has never died. The light is shining in the darkness and increasing, not diminishing. We can see that very distinctly.

A glorious future is destined for the Planet Earth. Those who are prophets can see it, and they are not few, but man himself must awake to the situation and become active. Anyone with ordinary intelligence can see that wars should cease, crime should cease, poverty should not be, cheating and chicanery should not exist.

The papers are full of distressing accounts of robbery, murder and rape in the cities, and war between the smaller nations in which the larger nations are implicated. But the population as a whole makes no effort to remedy the condition.

On every coin that is used by the people these words are clearly stamped, Liberty, In God We Trust, and E Pluribus Unum which means, From Many One. These words were in the hearts and minds of the founders of the nation and every child has heard them.

Now in this century of the Earth a great movement is spreading, beginning in the United States of America and spreading out in all directions to all parts of the globe. Groups of people are coming together to worship God, whose love and power are the basis of all creation. There are different ways in the various groups, of receiving and giving forth, that which in every case comes from the Great Spirit which is the cause of all life, love and peace.

Some groups practice decreeing, which is a repetition of phrases full of love, demanding cleansing of the Earth and its inhabitants, and replacing that which is untrue and destructive with Love and Truth. Other groups come together to receive teaching from Great Masters who speak through the leaders of the groups.

Besides the many groups there are individuals who are receiving the words of Truth from the higher realms of Life, and writing them to send out to all who are searching for Truth and illumination. There are many who are searching, and many who have found, for the time is now ripe. This small writing is given in that way. I, Mercury, receive the thought and the words from a higher Source, and the one who does the manual writing receives the words from me. It is very simple. With this writing much love is given, for love is that which accomplishes all good works. When there is love there is also light, and wisdom and joy are the result. The foundation of all is complete faith in the living Source of all, which in most countries is called God.

Whatever word may be used to designate this great force, it is one and the same force. That which is life everywhere, and love everywhere, expressing in all forms and creations. Life is the foundation, and love is the key, to all that is constructive, and we must not forget faith, which encourages and strengthens those who work in the vineyard of life. Faith is very necessary.

Beloved ones who read this little booklet. You are seekers for the Truth of life. Your hearts are full of love for humanity. Have faith in the Great Power which guides the destiny of every living being, be it man or little bird. The birds build their nests and raise their young ones by unthinking faith. Men accomplish marvels by thinking faith.

All great inventors have faith. Their faith is strong and unyielding. Disappointment after disappointment is conquered, and faith is still strong in their hearts. Sometimes the one who began the work does not succeed, but the work is taken up where he left off, by another worker in another generation.

All mankind is one. No one lives alone. It may seem so on the surface, but within all is one life. One energy pours through the whole; one great power, the power of love, holds all together as one.

This we on the Planet Mercury have learned by hard and bitter experience, for we had sunk to the depths as you on the Earth have done. Greed, war and destruction were rampant all over our planet. It became so bad that something had to be done. There is a saying on the Earth, "Mans extremity is God's opportunity."

This is true, and in desperation we turned to God for help. When I say we, I am speaking of the population of the planet and all, both population and ruler are one. I had done all I could to reach the hearts and minds of the people, and make them understand what was happening because of their greed. But they would not listen until they were in extremity.

Then they stopped, looked and listened. Then they asked for help. They raised their minds to the Source of their beings and prayed for help in their desperation, and help came. The Lord of all creation answered their prayers as He always does when prayers are sincere and unselfish. All troubles can be overcome by honest, sincere prayer. We urge man to listen to us and follow our example, for the result was even beyond our expectation.

Now you know why the people of the Planet Mercury are living lives of complete happiness, with plenty of the material goods necessary for physical sustenance, and all the beauty and joy of spiritual life.

Now that you have read this and understand something of the history of this planet, the next thing is for you to accept our invitation and visit us. When you travel over our planet, as our guests, visiting our towns, our factories, schools, libraries, and most important our private homes, you will be ready, when you return to the planet Earth, to begin in earnest to follow our example.

Theory alone is worthless – practice is needed in order to bring results. But before the people of Earth are ready to accept what I have been telling them and practice it on their planet, they must let us take their leaders in our ships to our planet as our visitors.

I will give you an idea of what is to be seen on our beautiful planet. Remember, it is a small planet and there is only one nation and one race. Our ship shall go directly to the capitol. It is a beautiful building, but not more beautiful than your capitol at Washington, D.C. We enter and find nothing very different from your capitol.

We leave and go to a court of law where a trial is under way. Here there is a striking difference. There is a judge and a jury but there are no lawyers. There are two men who have had a disagreement concerning a piece of property-about the boundary line between two homes. Each one was given an opportunity to speak, without interruption. A stenographer took down all that was said. Then the judge and the jury withdrew to another room which is called, "The room of consultation." There they discussed the situation, by first carefully reading the stenographic record, and then any member of the jury who wished to speak raised his hand and the judge called his name. He gave his opinion, which was taken down by the stenographer. If another disagreed, he was recognized by the judge, and he spoke.

This was continued until everyone who wished to express his opinion had done so. There was no oratory or flowery language, no effort to put either of the contestants in a bad light. All were calm and quiet in giving their opinions.

We with our visitors do not wait until the case is decided, for it will take some time to read all the records of the jurors' opinions. When all these have been studied the judge will give the deciding verdict. There has been no verbal fighting, no oratory, only quiet expressions of opinion. The judge is well versed in the law, for there are laws which are scrupulously followed. Sometimes, if there have been many contrary opinions by the jurors, it may be several days before the judge gives his verdict.

Now we shall get into our conveyance and go to another small town. We are not traveling in a space ship, but in a conveyance not very different in appearance from your automobile. However, there are differences. The fuel, like that of the space ship is drawn from the atmosphere and there are no noxious fumes pouring into the air. We drive out into the country over smoothly paved roads. There are beautiful trees, grass, and flowers in all directions. In the distance we see mountains whose tops are capped with snow. We pass through several small towns. The people live in pretty little houses, each individually planned. In front and around each there are flowers, and behind there are sometimes vegetables and fruit trees. Much of your own planet used to be like this, but there is not much like it now.

There is no large city anywhere on the planet Mercury. Even in these small towns there arc parks and playgrounds for children. Of course there are schools and shops. Everywhere the air is pure and sparkling and the sky blue, for it is not raining on the day we take you to visit us. We do have rain at times for without it the planet would be a desert. We have learned how to draw the clouds and produce rain when it is needed. It is said that your American Indians can do this, and the white people have occasionally brought rain from clouds that have gathered, but it is not regularly practiced.

There are not many restaurants or hotels m our towns, usually one of each, for that is enough to accommodate the travelers who are passing through. Our party goes to one of the hotels and finds it clean and comfortable. In another town we eat at the restaurant and find the food not very different from that to which you are accustomed.

But we have invitations from several, families, in different towns, who would like you to be their guests for a day and a night. You spend a day and a night with each one. Some of them have young children; others are older persons and have what you on Earth call teenagers. You have pleasant conversations with all these families, you eat their food, and you enter into some of their games and pastimes. They treat you like old friends, and you feel perfectly at ease and return their friendship.

We could fly easily from this planet and tour another planet but the plan for you is different. Your trips will all originate on the Earth and go to another planet each time, not from one planet to another. In this way you can judge the distance each planet is from your home planet, the Earth.

We all have strong hopes that you will accept our offer to teach you how to build a space ship like ours, so that you may travel from planet to planet and tour the entire solar system in a leisurely way. It will be like the tour of Europe, Asia or Africa that some of you fortunate ones make, not like a hasty guided tour of a few weeks, catching hasty glimpses of noted art galleries or beautiful scenery.

No, the plan is for you to linger long enough to really know the people and customs of each planet and make friends in each one. With your own ship you could do this. You could engage guides as you go from place to place. These would be professional guides such as there are in the countries of the Earth. They would know the history of the nation and all the places of interest on the planet and make friends in each one. With your own ship you could do this. You could engage guides as you go from place to place. These would be professional guides such as there are in the countries of the Earth. They would know the history of the nation and all the places of interest.

They would relieve you of all the troublesome part of travel, but you would not have to hurry, you could stay as long as you wished when you were interested, and if you were not interested, move on.

If you landed on a planet and found at once that you did not like it, you could enter your ship and be on your way to the next planet.

This is a carefully thought out plan, not only by the rulers of the planets, but by the Great White Brotherhood, which has communication with the people of Earth whose minds are open to them. They can prepare the minds of their students so that they can receive telepathic communication direct from us.

Any one of you could receive messages if you had the desire to do so and the love which would give the incentive. When you pray to your Father in heaven, you are both the sender and the receiver of a telepathic message. There is nothing supernatural about it, it is entirely natural.

We are also communicating with you by visiting you in our space ships. Many of you have seen these ships and some of you have conversed with those who are in them. There have even been instances when the Earth man has been taken on board and shown over the vessel, or in a few cases, actually taken to visit a planet. People are losing their fear and many are becoming very much interested in the ships which hover over the Earth or land upon it.

How beautiful the Earth could be, for it was very beautiful when it was a new creation. Think of the most beautiful landscape you have ever seen and imagine all of the Earth like that. All was like one big, glorified park. Man was put on this beautiful planet, told to increase and multiply, and to care for the Earth, the plants and animals.

Alas, the demon greed entered in, and now the soil is being poisoned and the animals and birds killed. Greed is the worst sin there is. It is the opposite to love. Love never destroys, it is always constructive. It is the cause of great inventions, beautiful pictures, delightful music; everything that brings happiness and peace. Greed is a destroyer and causes war and poverty.

We on the planet Mercury know this, not only in our minds, but in our whole beings, for we have experienced it ourselves. That is why we are so very anxious to warn our brothers on the planet Earth, and to urge them to listen to us, for we know that of which we are speaking.

Our love and blessings are always with the people of Earth, for we are all the children of the One Great Creator.

## THREE UNDISCOVERED PLANETS

This writing comes from a planet that has not been discovered by the powerful instruments of the astronomers. This planet is one of three which are not far from the planet Earth but are invisible to the human eye, even when looking through telescopes. The reason for this is because the planet and the inhabitants of the planet are not in flesh, as those who have communicated with you so far are. We are in etheric bodies, as are the souls of those who leave the physical body in so-called death.

I can assure you, however, that we are just as much alive as you are, really more alive. We are not ever troubled by sickness or weariness. We never tire. Our minds are keen and our hearts are full of love. We can travel any distance without a machine of any kind. In other words, our lives are lives of perfection.

171

You may wonder, then, how we can give ourselves as examples of living to the people of Earth. The planets that have spoken before are populated by those in physical bodies. They are living lives of happiness and peace and it makes them sad to see the tumult on the Earth, the struggle and war among nations, the greed among individuals.

I must admit that we, in our present state, cannot offer ourselves as examples to man, but we were centuries ago flesh and blood beings just as you are. We were sinful, greedy and grasping. Our bodies became sick, tired and weary, and we fought battles between nations and even civil wars within a nation.

Now all of us have passed through that which has been ignorantly called death. There is no death, only transition from one state of life to another.

We are all now in etheric bodies, which is another name for spiritual bodies. Our lives are entirely lives of love and peace. This does not mean that our lives are dull and uninteresting, far from it. Our lives are full of interest and activity.

This which I am doing now, writing to the planet Earth, is interesting and new to me. It is the first time I have spoken to an inhabitant of the Earth, so it is very interesting to me. On our own planet, even though it is my home, I am always finding something new and interesting. So never think that a life of peace and love must be dull.

Unhappiness, struggle and conflict are lacking and we are thankful that they are. The people of Earth could and can attain this peace and love, for within their physical bodies, spirit resides, and spirit is the true Self which lives forever. It is the Source of all Being. Spirit is the fountain of life where one may drink and live forever. Our great Teachers have taught us this, and we believe and within us know that this is true.

You people of Earth had a great Teacher who preached and lived this truth. He lived centuries ago and his name was Jesus. Many on Earth love him, but very few keep his precepts. We see the Earth in war and tumult, thousands suffer-ing from famine; starving in the cities and in the open country; marching in protest and revolt; destroying, stealing, killing.

How can this be? We would not believe that it could be true if we did not see it with our own eyes. We are able to see all that goes on at all times on our sister planet, Earth. Why do we speak of the other planets as "sister" instead of "brother"? Because the planets themselves are gentle, peaceful and loving no matter what the population may be.

Perhaps you have never known that a planet in itself is a living being, feeling, sensitive, loving. This is the truth. There is nothing in form anywhere that does not have life and feeling. In some forms the feeling is very dull, scarcely perceptible, in other forms, keen.

The planets are Beings of love and their feelings are keen. Their lives are passive. The lives of the inhabitants are not passive, they are very active, but they express peace, beauty and joy. They never do anything to destroy or injure the planet on which they live. The fauna of the planet is never destroyed, the animals are never killed.

Yes, there are animals, beautiful and gentle, and there are trees and flowers of great variety. There are mountains and valleys, lakes, streams and oceans. To look down from a distance and see this, one cannot see much difference from the planet Earth. Looking closer, however; there can be seen a great difference. There are no barren dry spaces where trees have once been. There are no deserts where the temperature is excessively hot, nor any place where the temperature is excessively cold.

Gentleness and peace reign everywhere. So it has been created, and so it remains. There are no wild beasts of prey. The animals are gentle, the birds sing and fly as yours do, but there are none preying on the smaller birds or little animals.

All living beings are Spirit, there are no beings of flesh and blood. This may seem very strange to the readers of these words, for to you Spirit is always invisible, that is, to the vast majority of the population; there are a few who are clairvoyant - clear seeing-who see at times the forms of the spirits.

Spirit is the pure essence of Life, proceeding from the Source of all Being. Flesh is only the container of Spirit. The body has been called the tabernacle of the Spirit. As such, it should be cared for and never abused. We, who are without flesh, nevertheless have form, and our forms resemble those of perfect men and women.

You all probably know that when a human being leaves the physical body he still has form, but the form is spirit, not flesh. He leaves the Earth for a higher sphere. It is easy to understand. With us, eons ago the entire population left the physical body, and the planet likewise abandoned the physical and existed only in the spiritual. It may seem very strange to you, but it can be understood.

There are three planets now living in spirit only and they are not very far from the planet Earth. Our planets, not being seen, have not been named by man. We have our own names in our own languages, for we have found it convenient to have language although we read minds usually.

Names are given for convenience, just as they are on Earth. The name of the planet on which I live is the name of a very beautiful flower which grows and blooms in profusion all over our planet. There is no way of giving it to you. It is the same with the other two planets; their names could not be spoken or written in your language or any other language.

The names are expressive of beauty in form, radiance and perfume. They are not all flowers, but they are all beautiful expressions of Life. We regret that we are unable to give these names to our sister planet Earth.

The writing of this booklet will be shared by all three planets, for though we are separate and individual our experience is similar and there would be nothing different to tell you.

All are planets of spirit living similar lives of love and happiness. Many of you on Earth receive communication from advanced Souls who speak to you from a plane above the Earth. They are in etheric bodies, though they have been men and women on the Earth.

The only difference in this communication is that I who speak have never been in physical body for it has been many eons in time since this planet and its inhabitants were in physical bodies. It is the same with the other two planets. Now I shall bid you beloved ones of Earth farewell and allow the other speakers to have their say.

This is the speaker of the next planet which is in spiritual form. There is nothing that I can add to my brother's talk. We are as like as two peas in a pod. You see we pick up some of your sayings.

This is only to say greetings and farewell and to assure you that we are your friends and well-wishers. I shall step aside and allow the brother from the third planet to greet you.

We are all now in etheric bodies, which is another name for spiritual bodies.
Spirit is the pure essence of Life, proceeding from the Source of all Being.

The gods were said to be tall and mighty and images of them were carved throughout antiquity. Photo by Tim Beckley.

## HERCULES AND THE SPACE GODS – AND THEIR RELATIONSHIP TO UFOs TODAY
### By Sean Casteel

**A**t a time when we need a real life "superhero" the most, we may have found one in the person of a Tenafly, New Jersey, gentleman who has dedicated himself to promoting some mighty hardcore beliefs in the supernatural and in the reality of parallel worlds that seemingly stretch back into infinity. Our hero has also been known to perform feats of strength and agility as well as demonstrating the power of mind over matter. In photos, he looks extremely well-muscled, a living example of the strongman ideal.

Over the years, Timothy Green Beckley, founder and CEO of the publishing house Global Communications, has assembled a crack team of writers. One of the more recent additions to Beckley's stable is paranormal experiencer and researcher Hercules Invictus, described above. True to his adopted name, Hercules is a follower of the ancient Greek gods of Olympus, who he believes are present here in the current age, concealing themselves behind masks more suited to our modern times.

For Hercules, belief in and contact with the gods began in his childhood.

Proudly, he says, "I am Greek and have recently begun the sixth decade of my current sojourn on Gaia. I was born into a culture that believed in the paranormal and I have had paranormal experiences since a very early age. The earliest paranormal memories that I can recall were from my crib. Aside from the continued presence of my physical family, I remember perceiving spirits, both human and nonhuman."

Today's Hercules complete with toga.

Hercules recalls three specific childhood experiences; portions of which he says were temporarily traumatic at the time.

"The first was when I initially encountered my Bear Totem," he said. "He is a fierce Spirit Animal that has protected me and guided me throughout much of my life, especially the first half. But when he first appeared in the waking world, I was terrified and cried out in terror. He quickly faded into the Dream Realm, where we slowly became friends.

"The second was when the Shadow People," Hercules continued, "who have interacted with my father's side of the family for generations and were very much a part of my early childhood, invited me to return with them to their world. I would have gone with them willingly, as they were my friends and playmates. Fortunately, a powerful Olympian presence intervened and informed me that, had I gone with them, I would have died in this world and would have been stuck in theirs."

The third experience happened while on a trip to the beach.

"I fell face down into the water," he said, "and was immediately transported into a strange undersea world full of frightening and fanciful creatures that I much later learned about in my mythic and folkloric studies. I felt like I belonged there and the sudden transition back to this world caused the trauma. My vocabulary was very limited at that time and years passed before I could share this experience."

The childhood experiences were the beginning of a lifetime of devotion to the paranormal as filtered through a heartfelt belief in the gods of Olympus.

"The gods of Olympus," Hercules affirmed, "are my ancestral deities and my affinity with them has been a constant throughout my life. Olympus provides me with a meaningful context for my life experiences and a transcendental purpose that resonates powerfully, thrills me and excites me."

The Olympians have always been active in our world, he says, and are still interacting with us today.

"They can be contacted in a variety of ways and will sometimes initiate contact in the physical world," he explained. "I myself have met several Olympians in the flesh and have spoken to them through their chosen vehicles or oracles. They also communicate through divination, visions, dreams, synchronicities and symbolism."

None of which, Hercules cautions, means that he worships the gods of Olympus.

"Though some moderns worship the Olympians," he said, "I personally do not. I honor them and endeavor to demonstrate that they are real and care about humanity through my actions in their name. The Olympians have never requested worship from me, nor do I encourage it for others."

Furthermore, there is no one true path or one true practice that leads to Olympian attunement or enlightenment. Hercules instead believes in something he calls "Olympian Pluralism," meaning there are many routes to the ultimate truth.

"Morals differ from place to place and from time to time," he added. "The Ancients, enlightened as they were in many ways, embraced many practices, like animal sacrifice, and institutions, like slavery, that we currently find extremely objectionable."

## THE PRIMAL VISION THAT GAVE HERCULES HIS NAME

As he was growing up, Hercules' parents would half-jokingly say that he belonged to Olympus and would return there after he died. His dedication to all things Olympian was cemented by a visionary experience in his childhood.

"When I was very young," he recounted, "a vision was implanted in my mind. I dubbed it my 'Primal Vision,' and can experience it instantly and vividly whenever I close my eyes. I have shared it openly throughout my life.

"I glimpse the top of a mountain, shrouded in mist," he begins. "Hovering on high, I can discern the ruins of an ancient acropolis in the timeless twilight. I wait alone, formless in the silence. In time, a lone figure, powerfully built and clad in the skin of a lion, makes his way towards the abandoned temple of 'The Highest.' His hair and beard are still mostly brown, though streaked with white and gray.

"In his right hand, he wields a knobby club studded with bronze. My consciousness enters this figure and henceforth I see through his eyes. I know that I am now Hercules, son of Zeus and progenitor of my line.

"Entering the fallen structure, I move through it unerringly until I reach a rectangular stone table, a long-neglected altar to the Olympians. Upon the altar is an antique horn, 'from a heavenly bull,' I tell myself. I then realize that I have been here many times before and I know exactly what I must do. The horn is of monstrous size and etched with arcane glyphs. Some of the etchings are inlaid with silver. I put down the club, cautiously lift the artifact to my lips, then blow into the smaller end with all my strength.

"The bellowing call echoes through the firmaments. With the Horn of Summoning still in hand, I exit the temple and peer purposely into the murky skies, near where I myself once hovered. I can detect faint presences, spirits that have answered my summons who will help me in carrying out my Olympian Mission. Some take of form, while others remain formless. But this I know: all who have responded will assist me in some unique and important way."

And with that realization, the vision begins to fade. Hercules is blessed with a brief glimpse of the ruins restored to their former glory. The sky is blue and clear, and there are mythic beings engaged in joyous activity, Hercules himself among them.

**Hercules is among the mighty gods residing on Mount Olympus to this very day.**

"I realize that this is Mount Olympus," he said, "my eternal point of origin and return, my Heaven and my soul's true home. As to my name, there is a term Greek, 'En Onomati Theou, which roughly means 'In the Name of God.' I dedicate myself completely to this particular Olympian, in all his guises, and I identify him as my Operant Archetype, Divine Pattern and Highest Self. Every action I undertake is thus a prayer and offering in his name."

Hercules further explained that his given name does not translate directly into English, but means something like "Dedicated to the Queen of Heaven." That queen's name in ancient times was Hera, and Hercules literally means "Dedicated to Hera" or "the Glory of Hera."

"Though I have been called by many names throughout my life," he said, "Hercules was always my default name and is now my legal name. I grew up during the Sword and Sandal era and loved the Hercules movies and cartoon. I've dressed up as the cinematic Hercules throughout my life and continue to do so, even now. I could never imagine, nor have I ever wanted, to be anything other than Hercules."

Hercules believes that the Olympians spoke to the early contactees and still speaks with folks as the denizens of other planets in our solar system and beyond.

## THE OLYMPIANS STILL SPEAK TO US

The Olympians still speak to us, as they always have.

"It has been my experience that the Olympians, who have assumed many guises in many cultures," Hercules said, "will communicate with you through the masks that you're most comfortable with. For many years, I played hide and seek with the gods as I explored the spirituality of different cultures through study and immersion. I would eventually find the same familiar faces behind the diverse cultural disguises.

"I believe that the Olympians spoke to the early contactees," he went on, "and speak with folks still as the denizens of other planets in our solar system and beyond it. And they are telling the truth. Astro-Mythology has been a viable vehicle of communication since the days of Babylon."

Hercules made reference to a book published by Timothy Green Beckley called "**Space Gods Speak**," which is a curious and underappreciated work that is nevertheless greatly valued by those who recognize what it is and can figure out how to use it.

The late female contactee "Tuella" was an important part of "**Space Gods Speak**." She established the Ashtar Command, a group of devotees dedicated to understanding the cosmic message delivered by the Space Brothers and to preparing for the eventual apocalyptic transition to a new and better world – the same paradise that Hercules called Mount Olympus when he saw it in his vision.

"I never knew Tuella personally," Hercules said, "but I had a close friend who was part of Tuella's Ashtar Command group for many years and frequently interacted with her. As Tuella was falsely rumored to have channeled '**Space Gods Speak**,' and later Tim Beckley identified the tome as '*An Ashtar Command Book*,' I wished to learn more. So I reached out, but Tuella had passed and my friend's spiritual journey had long since taken her elsewhere. Though I've interacted with more than a handful of Ashtar Command groups since the 1990s, nothing ever clicked.

"I have been a huge fan of Tim Beckley and his band of paranormal researchers for a big chunk of my life. I crossed paths with Tim back in the days when John Keel was hosting the Fortean Society in New York City. I reconnected with Tim when he was making low-budget horror movies. I sporadically stayed in touch during the intervening years. I am greatly honored to be in his company as a fellow adventurer and chronicler. This is a dream come true for me, and I am grateful for the opportunity to share the details of my journey."

## WHAT IT ALL MEANS

According to Hercules, it can be summed up this way:

"My current understanding is that the Olympians have guided many cultures and are known by many names. They care for their people, shape their destinies, and guide their evolution. Some of us are Vehicles or Vessels – embodied reflections of Olympus' Light, the Dream Selves of the Gods or their projections into this world.

"We have chosen to drink from the Waters of Forgetfulness, and enter the Dream of Mortality in order to assist in the Great Awakening on Gaia. Our purpose is to transcend and unravel the conditioning of our culture and awaken to our true Olympian nature, assuming our rightful place as co-creators of Elysium. Awake or asleep, we serve the purposes of Olympus.

"I am personally tasked with locating and liberating incarnate Olympians ensnared by the Dream of Mortality and reminding them of their Olympian mission. Mindful that archetypal Olympian patterns have been programmed into the human psyche, I believe in assisting all people on Gaia with actualizing their maximal potential. My efforts, whether couched in the language of myth or not, support all of humanity's efforts to transcend this world and venture forth into the great beyond, be those efforts metaphysical, mechanical or even imaginal.

"All of my Labors in this lifetime celebrate the Hero's Journey in myth, legend, spirituality, popular culture and in daily life. I firmly believe that the human spirit is essentially heroic and is always seeking ways to express its innate nobility and greatness. And that a life, fully lived, dedicated to actualizing the Highest we can conceive, is the noblest expression of human existence."

**EDITOR'S NOTE:** Hercules Invictus is a Lemnian Greek, a proud descendant of Argonauts and Amazons. He is openly Olympian in his spirituality and worldview, dedicated to living the Mythic Life and has been exploring the fringes of our reality throughout his entire earthly sojourn. For over four decades he has been sharing his Olympian Odyssey with others.

Having relocated the heart of his Temenos to Northeastern New Jersey and the Greater New York Metropolitan Area, he is now establishing his unique niche locally and contributing to his community's overall quality of life. Hercules is also recruiting Argonauts to help him usher in a new Age of Heroes.

Hercules currently hosts **The Elysium Project**, **Pride of Olympus** and **Voice of Olympus** e-radio shows on the **Spiritual Unity Radio Network**. He writes for **The Magic Happens**, **Paranormal Magazine** and **Paranoia Magazine**, has published two e-books on Kindle, **Olympian Ice** and **The Antediluvial Scrolls,** and has been contributing regularly to Timothy Beckley's anthologies.

Hercules founded or co-founded **Mount Olympus LLP**, **Olympian Heroic Path**, **Olympian Shamanic Path**, **Cosmic Olympianism**, **Mythic Atlantis**, **Living Theurgy**, the **Order of the Golden Fleece**, the **Regional Folklore Society of Northeastern PA** and the **Center for the Study of Living Myth** in New Jersey. He also spearheaded many of the real-world Age of Heroes initiatives and the fictive Mythic Adventure tales.

For more information, please Friend him on Facebook or visit his website: www.herculesinvictus.net

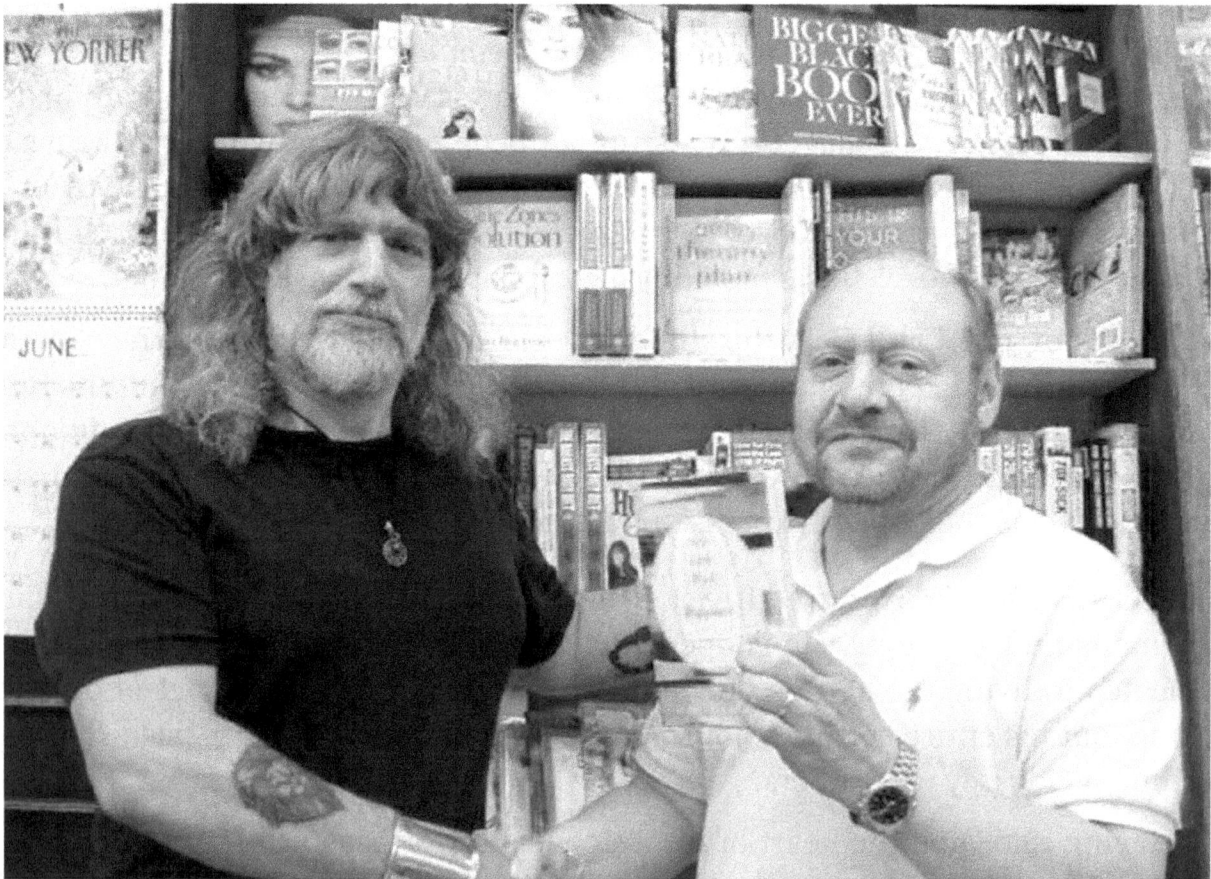

Hercules at Mayor's Wellness campaign, Tenafly, NJ.

(Illustration) UFOs have been seen around the ancient mystical sites of Greece to this day.

## SUGGESTED READING

*ASHTAR - REVEALING THE SECRET OF THE FORCES OF LIGHT*

## GLOBAL COMMUNICATIONS BOOKS TO WHICH HERCULES HAS CONTRIBUTED:

*THE SPACE GODS SPEAK: TRANSMISSIONS FROM THE SOLAR COUNCIL*

*WEIRD WINGED WONDERS*

*THE MATRIX CONTROL SYSTEM OF PHILIP K. DICK AND THE PARANORMAL SYNCHRONICITIES OF TIMOTHY GREEN BECKLEY*

*HIDDEN TREASURES OF THE KNIGHTS TEMPLAR*

*ALIEN STRONGHOLDS ON EARTH*

*GEF THE TALKING MONGOOSE*

We will come. We will land. We will make ourselves known.
We will take on board those who are worthy, those who are
aware of our presence, those who are involved in the New Age.

## ASHTAR'S END TIME NOTES

### By Timothy Green Beckley

*"SOMEDAY WE WILL ALL TRAVEL TOGETHER, ON THE SAME BEAM OF LIGHT,*

*TOWARD THAT ONE SOURCE."*

ASHTAR, FROM *"PROPHECIES FROM SPACE."*

Carol Ann Rodriguez was born and grew up in Queens, NY. She obtained a BA degree from The City College of New York and a Masters Degree in Education from Hunter College. She has a NY state teaching certification. During the early 1970s, while teaching preschool, Carol began studying at the New York School of Occult Arts and Sciences, where she met and studied the universal teachings of the Ashtar Command. She also studied art at Parson's School of Design and soon began to do illustrations for Inner Light Publications/Global Communications. Her works have also appeared in numerous other publications and books. She is perhaps the most prolific inspirational artist in the field today. Publisher Tim Beckley says her work is in the same league as the art of Peter Max with its many stars, planets and rainbows. Carol continues to do art as well as editing to the present as well as continuing her spiritual and metaphysical studies.

**N**eedless to say, it is not within the scope of this present publication to document all the many messages that have been channeled from Ashtar and other members of the various federations of planets that are said to exist throughout the vast universe. There are hundreds, perhaps thousands of messages floating around out there on the internet. But what, you might ask, could we offer in the way of proof that these disclosures are not the work of over-active imaginations? No scientific method is presently available to verify that which must for the present still be referred to as the supernatural or paranormal. We can only take each message or group of messages and test them out to our own satisfaction. When dealing with anything in the realm of the psychic it is always necessary to use a little of your own sensitivity to separate the wheat from the chaff.

Carol Ann Rodriguez along with Timothy Green Beckley.
Photo by April Troiani, with assistance from Big Earl.

Carol Rodriguez is a talented artist from New York, who has for quite a number of years remained actively interested in the subject of UFOs and in the possibility that humanlike space beings are monitoring our activities down here on earth. Her mind has remained open to new ideas and thoughts which others might reject out of hand simply because they might at first seem farfetched. Carol knows that anything is possible as she has experienced any number of psychic related manifestations in her life which have enabled her to draw the conclusion that other entities co-exist along with mankind in the same solar system in which we reside.

Over a period of years, Carol was present when a dedicated business professional saw fit to serve as a "go between" for the Ashtar Command. This individual refused to allow his identity to be made public since he believes it would hamper his ongoing work. "He doesn't find it necessary to go before the public," Carol explains, "as he feels the notoriety would only take away from the importance of the message and would place him in the spotlight instead of the actual source for this information, which must now be gotten out to the public at all cost."

In addition to being the one who has had the privilege of asking questions of Ashtar, Carol has also been of tremendous help in transcribing the tapes of the dozen or more communications that were beamed through this anomalous channel.

And while the messages from Ashtar have covered a wide variety of topics, Ashtar seems most anxious to get his specific thoughts across on the very subject we are so fascinated by, mainly the End Times.

The following notes have been taken directly from the cassette tapes hereby known as the Ashtar End Time Notes. Some editing for clarity sake has been done, but the essence remains true to the actual discourses. We have decided to present the material in a series of questions, followed by, in most instances, a most relevant answer. And while there are still missing pieces of the puzzle that we will fill in later on, these messages, I feel, go a long way in adding to our knowledge of the Last Days.

## WHEN WILL YOU LAND AND EVACUATE THE EARTH?

The time is not so far away. When that time does arrive, you and the other chosen ones will be taken up to a safe place in outer space. Perhaps this will be on some other planet, or a large mothership. From there you can watch your planet being destroyed. Should the end come through an explosion, a nuclear war (which we will do our best to prevent), we will monitor the radiation from space, and do the best we can to sweep your atmosphere clean so that those that have been chosen, and who have been taken up, can eventually be brought back to earth later on.

It is impossible to predict an exact date; however, things are leading up to a point where such an event cannot be postponed much longer. Your planet's vibrations are very, very negative. There are many forces on your planet that are seeking to control the destiny of millions and millions of people.

Things are bad. Things are disastrous. It could happen at any time. It could happen tomorrow. It could happen a week from now. It could happen a year from now, or five years from now. It is impossible to predict the exact date, but there are some things that will happen, some things that you can watch for and mark on your calendar.

## WHAT ARE SOME OF THESE SIGNS YOU SPEAK OF?

There will be a country in the Middle East that will be overtaken by the country you call the Soviet Union. When this happens the time will not be far off. When this happens the time will be close at hand. Such is happening now in Afghanistan, but it will spread.

The power of the Soviet Union is very mighty. They are very powerful. They have a great military machine. Your United States feels that it is the will of the people that we try to liberate these people living under the Soviet Union and the Communist Manifesto. While it is certainly brave and courageous that your government feels this way, it is also leading you down the path to a nuclear holocaust.

The two forces are opposing. They are like magnets, magnets that repel each other, and this can only lead to a catastrophe. It is too bad that this has to happen. We would like to see it avoided, but it will be difficult to do so. You have built your military up to the point where both nations could, very easily, destroy themselves through a nuclear holocaust. There is no backing out now, it seems. Both countries are very influential in the world. The next war could possibly be a very disastrous one. Millions of people will be killed, millions of people will be slaughtered but some - the lucky ones - will be saved.

We will come. We will land. We will make ourselves known. We will take on board those who are worthy, those who are aware of our presence, those who are involved in the New Age.

## IF THERE WERE A NUCLEAR HOLOCAUST, WOULDN'T THIS CAUSE PROBLEMS IN OUTER SPACE? WOULDN'T THE ENTIRE SOLAR SYSTEM BE AFFECTED?

Yes, this is true. You see, if there were a nuclear holocaust on your planet, it would cause a vibration like a chain reaction that would vibrate through the entire solar system and would cause negative effects. It might cause, not only a disturbance in your polar alignment, but it could also cause this to happen on several other planets. It is possible indeed and so we have to watch you with keen interest. Not only do we not want you to destroy yourselves, but we don't want to see any of our other brothers throughout the solar system destroyed either.

## CAN'T YOU DO SOMETHING TO STOP THESE THINGS FROM HAPPENING?

We are doing what we can at this time. There are people amongst you who are from the various planets in the solar system and they are trying to get to your leaders, trying to get them to see the situation they are getting into. But it is really impossible to change the minds of individuals. Though we can alert them to the facts, though we can try to shine the light of universal love on them, it is impossible if their will is not strong enough to want to change. For you see there is not just one leader on your planet. Your own President for example, he does not have the power.

The power is given to many. It is given to the scientist. It is given to the military. This is true not only in the United States, but also in other countries. Not one person holds the key to peace. If this were the case, we would probably come down and take him away and all would be well. It is true that some are willing to listen. Many others refuse to as it is their own greed that they are looking out for, not the welfare of their own people, or the welfare of space people throughout this solar system.

## CAN YOU TELL US MORE ABOUT THE HOLOCAUST?

There will be a natural holocaust that will take place, caused, not only by the nuclear explosions of war, but because your own weather, your own atmosphere, is so rapidly changing. You have already seen this with the repeated eruptions of the volcano you call Mount St. Helens in Washington state, but there will be others that will be taking place around the world. There will be an increase in earthquakes and volcanic eruptions, and these will also cause many related disasters and loss of life. These are all signs the time is near, that times are changing, that your whole planet is going through a change.

We would like to see these things not happen as they would be bad for all of us. But it is impossible to change the course of history. We could look, we could observe, we could do what we can, but we cannot change the facts.

You have created your own life, your own civilization, and it is impossible for us to come down and actually interfere. This would be against the universal laws. We might even be able to give you advice, but if you do not listen it is not up to us to prevent these things. This is a natural occurrence, something you have brought upon yourselves, and you will have to pay the karmic consequences.

There will be more signs in the heavens. Mankind will look to the stars for their salvation. All this will happen shortly. Within the next few years there will be many, many changes taking place on your planet. We are watching from far above, keeping tabs on your activities. We are hoping, we are praying, that these events do not transpire.

## COULD ANY OF THIS STILL BE AVERTED? IS THERE A PRAYER FOR MANKIND?

Yes, there is a chance this can all be averted, but with each passing day, that chance gets less and less. If mankind could change the way it lives, if mankind were to put down its arms, then it could be averted. However, there is no sign that this will happen.

Some day someone will take matters into their own hands and will push the button, the button that will end civilization as you have come to recognize it.

Look to the sky. Tell those that you know who believe, to look up, that we are coming in greater numbers. We will do what we can. Tell those who believe, tell those who are righteous, that we are here, that we are watching over them, that we are praying for their safety.

There will be many signs to look for. The signs will differ depend- ing upon what part of the earth you live on. When the earthquakes and volcanic eruptions start en masse, your sun and your moon will look different than they do now. There will be strange atmospheric conditions - a pink haze in the sky. This pink haze will cover everything so that when you see the moon, and when you see the sun, they will no longer appear the same to you. Also, the course of mighty rivers will be altered. One in South America will make headlines within the next few months. There will be a considerable number of earthquakes, some of which will even occur in your eastern United States. Though they have occurred before, this is the first time that such tremors of a very strong magnitude will be recorded.

## IS NEW YORK GOING TO BE DESTROYED?

New York has already destroyed itself. As for a total physical destruction, this may occur, but there is a strong possibility that it will not, for it would take a very strong physical reaction to sink or tilt the island of Manhattan. This may occur before the end as we know it, but by that time, most of the people will already be evacuated who will be taken off the planet.

## ARE THERE AREAS ON OUR PLANET WHICH WILL BE SAFE TO LIVE IN FOR AT LEAST A LITTLE WHILE?

There will be areas which you can go to that will be safe. Arizona is one such place that is frequently mentioned, and it is a good place. Also Wyoming, Oklahoma, and perhaps the Dakotas.

You will know that the time has arrived to leave where you are when there is an increased number of UFOs seen in the sky. During the period just before the End Times, UFOs will be coming down here from many sources to watch these things, and at some point to lift off those people whose deeds are such that it makes it essential that they be taken along. These are the ones that we would have repopulate the earth at some future date. Also to be taken, are those that have particular skills or abilities and have no criminal record.

## HOW MANY PEOPLE WILL BE TAKEN FROM THE EARTH?

Each group coming down here will be taking people off. Our own ships will be responsible for upwards of 20,000. We would estimate that altogether perhaps 140,000 to 170,000 people will be lifted up and taken off the planet.

## THIS IS NOT VERY MANY CONSIDERING THE POPULATION OF THE WORLD

It is certainly true that this is not a great figure, but if the people on earth lived more according to the universal laws, the great catastrophes and holocaust would not take place. So why should we remove them, only to have the same thing start all over again? Also, the question arises if we were to take more than this, what would we do with these people? We would be responsible for their safety, for housing them, feeding them, and taking care of their various needs while they are away from the planet. It would be anywhere from five years to several decades before the earth is safe to be repopulated again. After the Great War, if one should occur, we will send ships down that will clear the air of any radioactivity. The volcanic eruptions will probably simmer down in awhile. The earthquakes will also become less frequent because there will be a shifting, probably of the entire earth's axis. So the whole land mass will be reshaped entirely. There will be very few areas that will be able to stand the force of the holocaust. These few safe areas that we mentioned will only be safe in the beginning, as when the earth tilts on its axis, if that is what is to happen, whole land masses will be completely altered. But, it is from these areas that a good many of the people that will be picked up will be lifted off the earth.

## WHERE WILL THESE PEOPLE BE TAKEN TO?

There will be several large cities in space, some of which your scientists have already observed. These ships which can house many, many thousands of people will be put in orbit around the sun as if they were planets themselves. Then at the time the earth has been made stable again, the people will be brought back. These planets orbiting around the sun will be big enough so that people can go on living quite comfortably. Food will be grown there. There will be recreation and entertainment areas. There will be schools. There will be hospitals. Life will go on.

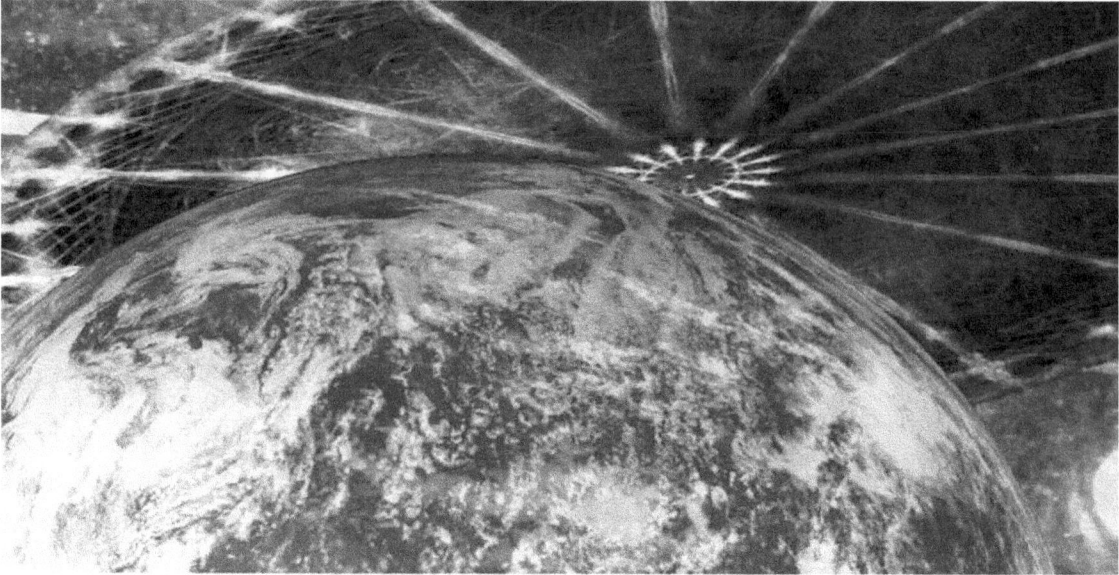

You will know that the time has arrived to leave Planet Earth when there is
an increased number of UFOs seen in the sky.

If you watch the news you can see that the earth is like a festering wound, a wound that keeps getting larger and larger. There is more hatred among mankind than ever before. The bomb is about ready to explode. But do not fear, be happy, be content, be glad that you are living in such an important era. And remember, watch the skies for we are here and we are watching over you. We send our love, we send our well wishes, we send our strength and our power to you and those who are deserving.

## IF OUR LEADERS WERE TO ACKNOWLEDGE YOUR EXISTENCE COULD YOU IN ANY WAY BE ABLE TO ASSIST US?

Your planet would jump many years ahead in technology if your scientists and world leaders would simply acknowledge our presence. We have many things we would like to share with you that we could teach you, that you could learn from.

At this very moment, your energy, the energy that you have within the bowels of the earth, is depreciating. Very, very soon there will not be enough power for your cities to provide you with the energy you need for heat, for refrigeration.

The economics are very, very bad, not only in your own country, but in other countries as well. There are many unstable conditions which we could help improve.

And while these are troubled times, these are also good times for those who will open their minds, for those who would cast their eyes skyward, for those who look for our gleaming craft. For we come with knowledge, with love and peace in

194

our hearts. It is very important that your world unite, for separated as it is now, it will eventually destroy itself. Unity is important.

One of the reasons that we are making select contacts at this time is to tell you that your planet cannot stand another world war. In a world war there would be no winner, every side would be the loser.

## YOU MEAN NO ONE WOULD SURVIVE THE END TIMES HERE ON EARTH?

More than likely there will always be people on the earth. These catastrophes will take the lives of millions, but there will always be places for people to hide. In fact, there are now people who are living underground, people who are actually living inside your own planet, who once lived on the surface many eons ago. But they too nearly destroyed themselves. Some of them built rocketships to go into outer space, while others built cities underground.

UFOs are very important. We ask that you get the word out. We ask that you tell as many people as possible about the existence of flying saucers, for they are very important for your state of development. Readers should note that a portion of the above channeled communications have been excerpted from the text "*The New World Order: Channeled Prophecies From Outer Space,*" now out of print, as originally issued by Inner Light Publications in a limited edition.

## <u>SUGGESTED READING</u>

**PLEASE NOTE** – Interested parties can now get all the transmissions in a fully updated version "*Cosmic Revelations Till The End Of Time: Channeled Prophecies From The Galactic Guardians.*"

For other interesting books and fascinating items, write for our FREE catalog.

Global Communications

P.O. Box 753

New Brunswick, NJ 08903


Email: mrufo8@hotmail.com


Conspiracyjournal.com

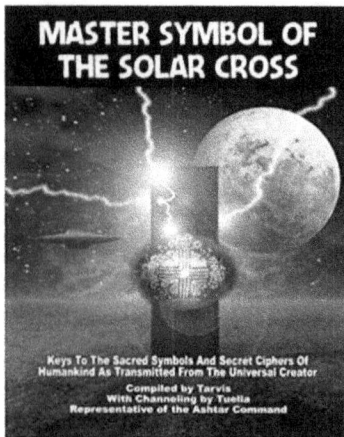

## Master Symbol Of The Solar Cross

HERE ARE THE SECRET MASTER KEYS TO THE GREAT AWAKENING FOR THE FIRST TIME THE SPIRITUAL HIERARCHY EXPOSES THE UNIVERSAL LAWS OF...LIFE – MAGNETIC RESONANCE – ACTION AND REACTION – LIGHT -- VIBRATION – MIND – HARMONY – DIMENSIONS – LOVE – POLARITY – ATTRACTION – MANIFESTATION. The primary channel for the Ashtar Command reveals the hidden Sacred Symbols and Secret Ciphers of humankind as transmitted from the Universal Creator at this imperative time in the history of our planet...The Solar Cross symbolizes the developing relationship of our awareness to reality, which is all encompassing...In ancient history, sacred symbols were used in teaching all the basic principles of nature. Everything was taught in the simplest, most comprehensive language of symbols.
Large Format  $29.00

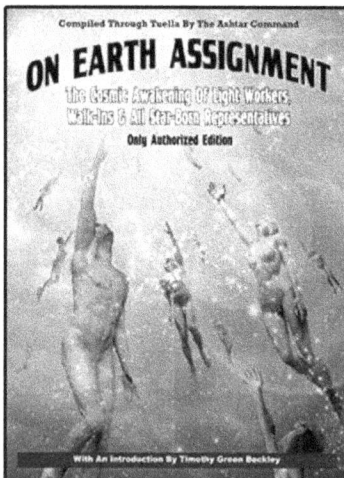

## On Earth Assignment: The Cosmic Awakening of Light Workers, Walk-Ins & All Star: Updated

The planet earth at this time is heavily populated with Ambassadors from far flung vistas of our Universe, a vast corps of volunteers. These dedicated ones are here on heavenly assignments to aid the coming of Light and Understanding to mankind, enduring the limitations of fleshly existence to fulfill that ideal. Are you one of them? They are the "seed souls" through whom great ideals are transferable, incorporated within creative personalities through whom the past and future become integrated.

Light workers unite – the time has almost arrived. According to the Ashtar Command you have been born upon this planet at this specific time in order to help in humankind's spiritual development. Some of you have arrived from a far distant star systems. Others may be reincarnated from Atlantis, Mu or Pan to assist in a cosmic plan that is long in the making. Many do not realize yet what their assignment is, while others are just starting to see the veil lifted as their consciousness starts to expand in a more cosmic direction. Do you feel you are an "outsider?"That something is adrift in your life, that there has to be more meaning to "all of this?" Do you love nature? Animals? All of Gods creations equally? Do you see through the sinister plot by certain greedy elements of society to keep us enslaved as a species so that we can be kept under the master's thumb? This book is not meant for everyone – far from it! It is meant for those who feel they have been "chosen" for a mind altering opportunity that will help to lead those who are worthy to a new place among the stars. Your time is here Starchild – REJOICE! – Large Format - $19.95

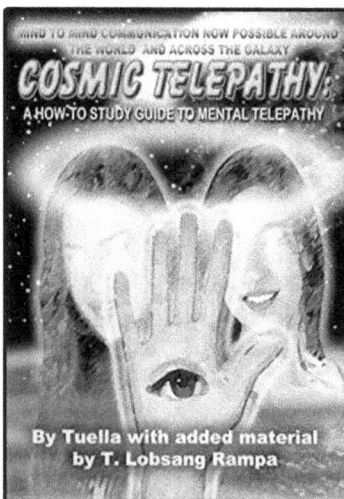

## Cosmic Telepathy: A How-To Guide To Mental Telepathy

A SIMPLE HOW TO PERSONAL EMPOWERMENT BOOK PRESENTED IN AN ORGANIZED BOMBARDMENT OF SPIRITUAL TRUTH. . . EXPERTS PROCLAIM: MIND TO MIND COMMUNICATION IS NOW POSSIBLE AROUND THE WORLD AND ACROSS THE GALAXY. Shrouded in secrecy since ancient times, now it is possible for all sincere individuals to tap into that 80 percent unused portion of the human brain that will eventually enable humankind to cross the barriers of space and time, link up with our "cosmic cousins" and break down the walls of false illusion that exist between many races and groups on Earth. This vital workbook and study guide to expanding your clairvoyant and telepathic powers has been compiled by two of the foremost authorities on altered states of human awareness. TUELLA is widely recognized as the primary channel for the ASHTAR COMMAND, a galactic spiritual force that for decades has rendered valuable assistance in providing "shortcuts" guaranteed to bring about the removal of the wraps of secrecy and unnecessary ritual that have kept clairvoyant abilities out of the hands of the average person Written with T. Lobsang Rampa.  Large Format – $25.00

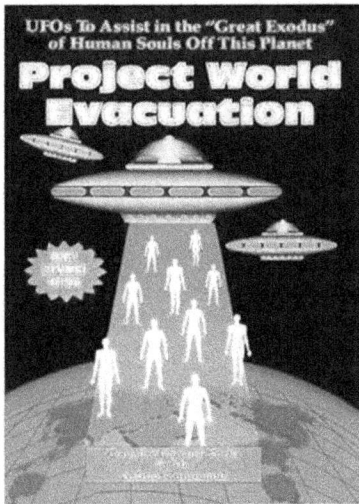

## Project World Evacuation: UFOs to Assist in the "Great Exodus" of Human Souls Off This Planet

THIS IS THE ONLY OFFICIAL EDITION OF THIS BOOK BY THE ASHTAR COMMAND -- AS TRANSFERED TO THE PUBLISHER BY TUELLA SHORTLY BEFORE HER PASSING. The primary channel for the Ashtar Command, Tuella's calling as a Messenger of Light began in the early seventies with her channeling worked commissioned personally on behalf of the Intergalactic Space Confederation. Says the channel: "Just as many are called and few are chosen, likewise many who read this book will neither understand nor receive the information. But those special souls for whom it is intended will rejoice in its guidance and accept its timely and imperative revelations." This information is not not entertainment. It is comparable to sealed orders given to dedicated volunteers on a strategic mission. It is dispersed to them, compiled for them and will be cherished by them. It is neither defended nor justified. It is data recorded as given and passed to those for whom it is intended. "Here is details of the three evacuations: * Understanding the three phrases of the Evacuation schedule. * Who will qualify? * Summary of what to expect. * The planned departure of the children. * What does the"Boarding Pass" consist of? * Total evacuation in 15 minutes. * Where will the rescued be taken? *The cause and effects of planetary acceleration. *Three months the earth will stand still...AND MUCH MORE!
Large Format – $19.95

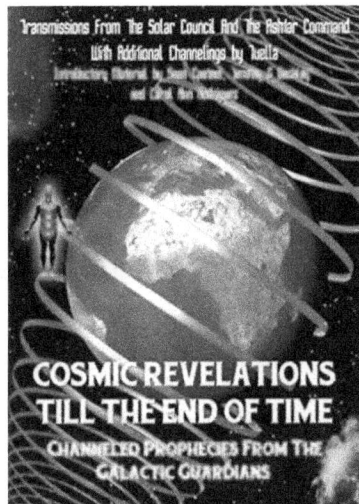

## Cosmic Revelations Till The End Of Time: Channeled Prophecies From The Galactic Guardians

In a series of telepathic "broadcasts," from a highly intelligent being who identified himself as Ashtar, Commander of a huge spaceship orbiting Earth, we are given prophetic revelations on a variety of relevant subjects, including: *The folly of our political systems. *The TOP-SECRET mission of the Space Brothers. *Spiritual development of humankind. *The selection of the "Chosen Ones" to be removed from the planet in event of a global disaster. *The inside of our planet is really inhabited. *Physical changes to be undergone by the planet in years to come. *Meditation key to lifting our vibrations. *Educational craft orbiting Earth. *Negative beings have infiltrated the military and government. *More assassination attempts to be made on world leaders. *The coming of open relations between Earth and other worlds. *Teleportation soon to be commonplace. *True meaning of "the beast" whose number is said to be 666. *Earth is a living entity. *Life in other dimensions.

BONUS TWO BOOKS IN ONE – ALSO CONTAINS AMAZING "COSMIC PROPHECIES" CHANNELED THROUGH TUELLA, PRIMARY REPRESENTATIVE FOR THE FREE FEDERATION OF PLANETS.
Large Format -- $19.95

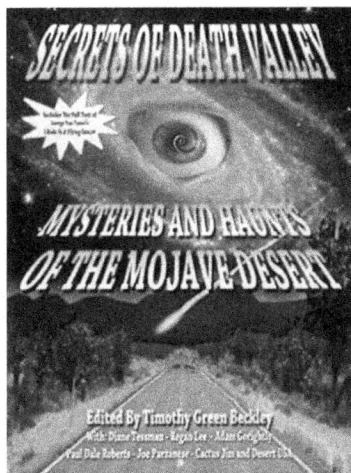

## Secrets Of Death Valley: Mysteries And Haunts Of The Mojave Desert (Includes Full Text of I Rode In A Flying Saucer)

Contains the first known transmissions from the Ashtar Command, early 1950s as received by George Van Tassel, as he went into a light trance under Giant Rock. This has to be one of the most magical looks at one of the most mystical places in North America. So many strange things have happened here that the Mojave has gotten a reputation for the place to go should an individual wish an authentic UFO or spiritual experience...As early as the late 1940s disc shaped craft were being seen by credible witnesses. And some like George Van Tassel professed to have been go for a ride on board a flying saucer...In fact, Van Tassel's messages from alien beings are included in a part of the book, making this even a more important collectors edition.
Large Format – $19.95

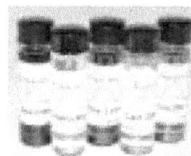